RANGE ROVER
(CARBURETTOR MODELS)
1970-1986
OWNERS' AND BUYERS' GUIDE

by James L. Taylor

1993
Published and distributed by
Yesteryear Books
60 Woodville Road
London NW11 9TN
(081-455 6992)
ISBN 1 873078 09 9

CONTENTS

Introduction	3
The marque	4
Development	5
Configuration	7
The Range Rover, 1970 to 1972	10
Buying a 1970-1972 Range Rover	13
The Range Rover, 1973 to 1979	15
Buying a 1973-1979 Range Rover	18
The Range Rover, 1980 to 1981	19
Buying a 1980-1981 Range Rover	21
The Range Rover Monteverdi	22
Buying a Monteverdi	24
Range Rover In Vogue, 1981	25
Buying a Range Rover In Vogue	27
Two-door and four-door Range Rovers, 1982	28
Buying a 1982 Range Rover	30
The 1983 Range Rovers	31
Range Rover Automatic In Vogue Special Edition, 1983	32
Buying a 1983 Range Rover	33
The 1984 Range Rovers	34
Range Rover In Vogue, 1984	36
Buying a 1984 Range Rover	36
The 1985 Range Rovers	37
Buying a 1985 Range Rover	40
The 1986 Range Rovers	41
Buying a 1986 Range Rover	42
Police-specification Range Rovers	43
Export Range Rovers	44
Modifications	45
Specifications - Home Market Range Rovers	49
Vehicle identification	50
Sales figures	53
Colour Chart	54
Miscellanea	55
Performance Figures	58

Range Rover
(Carburettor Models)
Owners' and Buyers' Guide
1970 - 1986
First published in 1993 by Yesteryear Books, 60 Woodville Road, London NW11 9TN
ISBN: 1 873078 09 9
© James Taylor, 1992

INTRODUCTION

The earlier examples of one of today's most prestigious road (and off-road) vehicles can afford an enormous amount of pleasure - but they can also inflict an enormous amount of damage on your wallet unless you buy wisely. The main purpose of this book, therefore, is to help would-be owners of a Range Rover to buy and enjoy an early example of one of these vehicles.

Although today's Range Rover is closely related to the models dealt with in this book, it is also a very different animal in many ways. In the mid-1980s, a series of radical changes redeveloped the vehicle to suit the prestige and luxury markets, and the basic simplicity of the original Range Rover was lost with the arrival of fuel injection and sophisticated electrical gadgetry. Those newer, more complicated vehicles, will deserve a book to themselves one day; but, for the moment, here is one devoted to those Range Rovers which can be looked after and rebuilt easily by the average DIY owner.

Range Rovers, like Land Rovers, are very rarely "standard", because owners tend to modify them in use. When buying a vehicle, it can be helpful to know what is "standard" and what is not, for the simple reason that the factory's Workshop Manual and Parts Book will not provide assistance on non-standard items. Far better to recognise from the outset how much of a problem this is likely to be than to find out the hard way when the vehicle breaks down! This book therefore aims to establish "standard" specifications, both to help those who

aim to keep a vehicle in original condition and those who need to establish exactly what has been modified on a vehicle.

The format chosen for this guide is a chronological one. It traces the development of the Range Rover between 1970 and 1986, when all models had carburetted 3.5-litre petrol engines. Each stage in the vehicle's development is discussed in detail, with specification changes and other useful points. After each of the descriptive sections comes a detailed guide on the strengths and weaknesses of the models in question. The advice it contains is designed not only to assist buyers in their choice of model, but also to warn them about potentially expensive faults. However, because major items like engine or gearbox are dealt with only once (on their first introduction), it is important to read the whole book and not just the section relating to a model of particular interest.

Many Range Rovers formed the basis of specialist conversions when they were new, and there is a section in this book devoted to them. Equally, many DIY owners have modified vehicles to suit their requirements, and there is a section on such modifications. Finally, the book includes some helpful specification tables and statistical data which will be of interest to the Range Rover owner.

Although neither the author nor the publisher can accept any liability for acts carried out on the advice given in this book, both would be pleased to be informed of any errors or omissions it contains.

December 1992
James L. Taylor

Many thanks to Land Rover Ltd *for help with information and pictures used in this book.*

Range Rovers have always been built at the Rover factory in Solihull. However, the ownership of this factory - and hence the identity of the vehicle's manufacturer - has changed several times.

By the time the Range Rover was launched in 1970, the old Rover Company which had initiated its development had been absorbed into the British Leyland Motor Corporation. Early vehicles were therefore built by Rover-British Leyland UK Ltd. There were several internal re-organisations over the next few years, but Range Rover "ownership" was not affected until November 1975, when Rover and Land-Rover manufacture fell to the new Leyland Cars subsidiary of what was now called British Leyland Ltd. In July 1978, Land Rover Ltd was formed as an autonomous company within British Leyland. Saloon car manufacture was separated from the four-wheel-drives in 1982, when Land Rover Ltd took over the whole of the Solihull site and British Leyland became the Austin Rover Group. In July 1986, right at the end of the period covered by this book, the company changed its name yet again - to Rover Group - but Land Rover Ltd remained unaffected.

The BL flying wheel logo, current when the Range Rover was announced in 1970.

The Leyland Cars version of the BL logo, current from 1975 to 1978.

After the creation of Land Rover Ltd in 1978, the company adopted this oval logo, with cream lettering on a green background.

DEVELOPMENT

Few people realise that the Range Rover story goes back as far as 1964, when the Rover Company sent a marketing specialist, Graham Bannock, out to the USA. Bannock's brief was to look at what Americans were buying, and to make recommendations which would enable Rover to expand its sales there. One of the conclusions which he brought back was that there was a developing market in recreational 4x4s in the USA. Rover's own experience of 4x4 manufacture would obviously stand it in good stead if it chose to enter this market.

What Bannock had seen was a market which had been largely stimulated by the 1961 launch of the International Scout, and in particular of its Travelall estate variant. This had been followed swiftly in 1962 by the Jeep Wagoneer, another large 4x4 estate. Then, in 1965 Ford brought out its Bronco, and in 1967 Chevrolet followed up with the Blazer. As what Bannock had predicted became reality in the mid-1960s, so Rover's thoughts about producing a

vehicle which might compete in this market sector began to crystallise.

The first sketches for what was to become the Range Rover were made in the early months of 1966. However, they did not originate on the Land-Rover side of the company. Rover's structure at the time was such that all major new vehicle projects were initiated by the same high-powered design team, whether the new vehicle was to be a car or a Land-Rover, and so it was that Tom Barton's Land-Rover engineers were not called in until a later stage in the proceedings.

The first significant step forward was made when Spen King, then head of the New Vehicle Projects team, proved to himself that the best ride characteristics for both on-road and off-road work could be obtained with low spring rates and long-travel suspension, such as were already fitted to the Rover 2000 saloon car. The second step came a few months later when the newly-acquired 3.5-litre V8

This clay model, dating from 1967, shows a Styling Department proposal for the Range Rover which was not adopted. Most striking are the car-like lines; even this early, Rover was well aware that its new vehicle would be more than just another Land Rover.

The styling of the first Range Rover was remarkably similar to that which eventually went into production. The most obvious changes were to the front end and to the lower body swage line.

engine, earmarked for saloon car use only at first, was made available to other Rover departments. This would provide the power needed for on-road performance plus the torque needed for off-road work, and was a far better choice than the 3-litre straight six which the New Vehicle Projects team had been considering up to that point.

With the V8 in the specification, the new vehicle began to look a lot more promising, and New Vehicle Projects were authorised to go ahead with serious design work. This caused a certain amount of irritation on the Land-Rover side of the house, where the engineers believed that only they knew enough about cross-country vehicles to design a new one, but their pleas went unheeded and they were simply instructed to second three engineers to the New Vehicle Projects team. By the end of the year, designer Gordon Bashford had come up with what looked like a reasonably definitive layout for the vehicle. This had a wheelbase of 99.9 inches, but Bashford suggested rounding the figure up, and the project was thereafter known as the Land-Rover 100-inch Station Wagon.

Over the next three and a half years, seven prototypes of the 100-inch Station Wagon were built, but its basic specification changed very little from these original plans. Similarly, although David Bache's stylists added some subtleties which gave the vehicle a classic timelessness, the actual shape of the body changed hardly at all from the original drawn up by Bashford and King with some assistance from Geoff Crompton of the Rover Styling Department. At the end of 1968, the vehicle was given the new name of Range Rover and then, at the insistence of British Leyland's Chairman, Lord Stokes, development was speeded up so that the vehicle could be introduced ahead of schedule.

CONFIGURATION

The basic configuration of the Range Rover remained constant for all the models covered by this book. Right from the beginning, the vehicle was built on a box-section chassis similar in general concept to that which had been drawn up in 1947 for the Land-Rover. Like the Land-Rover, the Range Rover also had beam axles, as experiments at Solihull had shown independent suspension systems were not compatible with good off-road ability. However, the Range Rover had two important features which the Land-Rover never had: long-travel coil spring suspension and four-wheel servo-assisted disc brakes. Both were intended to make the vehicle behave more like a car on the road and less like a small truck. An additional refinement was a Boge Hydromat self-levelling suspension strut at the rear, which helped the vehicle maintain normal handling when heavily laden.

The Range Rover's drivetrain was also very different from that seen in Land-Rovers before 1970.

For a start, it used a much more powerful engine than any seen in Land-Rovers. This was the 3½-litre all-alloy V8 which Rover had bought from the Buick division of General Motors in 1964 and had redeveloped to suit its luxury saloons. The first production application of the Rover V8 was in the 3.5-litre saloon and coupé introduced in autumn 1967, and the smaller Three Thousand Five followed soon after in April 1968. In most markets, however, these engines had a high compression ratio which demanded 100-octane petrol, a commodity which was not available in many of the overseas markets where Rover hoped to sell the Range Rover. For that reason, the engine was redeveloped with a lower compression ratio so that it would run on 91-93 octane petrol.

On Land-Rovers, two-wheel drive was normally employed for road driving, with four-wheel drive being engaged only to give extra traction in the rough. However, an axle capable of taking all the

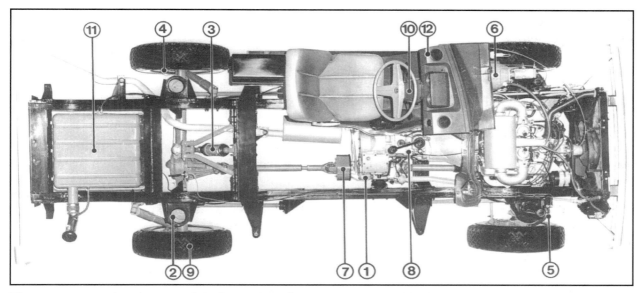

This picture, issued at the time of the Range Rover's announcement in 1970, shows the key features of its layout. They were:
1. *Centre differential*
2. *Coil springs on the beam axles*
3. *Boge self levelling strut on the rear axle*
4. *Disc brakes on all four wheels*
5. *Dual hydraulic lines to the front brakes*
6. *Servo-assisted brakes*
7. *Drum for the transmission parking brake*
8. *Four-speed, all synchromesh primary gearbox*
9. *Radial ply tyres*
10. *Collapsible "safety" steering column*
11. *19-gallon fuel tank*
12. *Impact-absorbing facia*

This close-up of the rear suspension shows the long-travel coil springs, the Boge ride-levelling unit, one of the "staggered" dampers, with one ahead of the axle and one behind, and the deep box-section chassis frame.

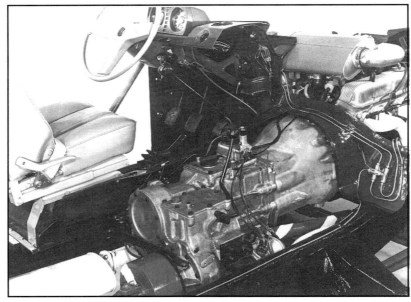

This demonstration cutaway clearly shows the layout of the transmission, with the two-speed transfer box in a casing alongside the rear of the primary gearbox.

V8's torque after multiplication through the low ratio of the transfer box would have been a tough and heavy component which would have increased unsprung weight to the detriment of ride comfort. As a result, the Range Rover was designed to have permanent four-wheel drive, so that the engine's torque could be split between two relatively light axles. For off-road work, a centre differential apportioned the torque appropriately between the two axles. A side benefit of the permanent four-wheel drive was that it also improved on-road handling in slippery conditions.

To meet the new crash-safety regulations which had been introduced during 1968 in the USA, (one of the Range Rover's intended markets), the vehicle needed a strong body shell. The inspiration for the design of this came from the Rover 2000 saloon, which consisted of a rigid "base-unit" to which the running gear and unstressed skin panels were bolted. The Range Rover's body shell was thus built up as a strong steel skeleton and, in order to make it suitable for CKD assembly, it was designed as a number of sub-units which were simply bolted together to make the complete shell. To this were then bolted unstressed skin panels of the same Birmabright aluminium alloy which had been used for Land-Rover bodies since the beginning. This had the advantage of being both light in weight and corrosion resistant. Bonnet and tailgate panels had to be more rigid to withstand heavier use, however, and so these were made of steel.

As a two-door body shell was quicker to develop than a four-door type, and as the main American four-wheel drives in the market at which the Range Rover was aimed had only two doors, no four-door shell was considered before 1971. Even then, it would be ten years before it would go into production! One penalty of the two-door configuration was that conventionally-mounted seat belts were likely to hinder access to the rear, and so the Rover engineers developed a completely new system in which the belts were anchored to a strong seat frame, itself firmly anchored to the body shell. These belts continued on two-door models throughout the period covered by this book, although later four-door models had a conventional upper belt mounting on the B-pillar.

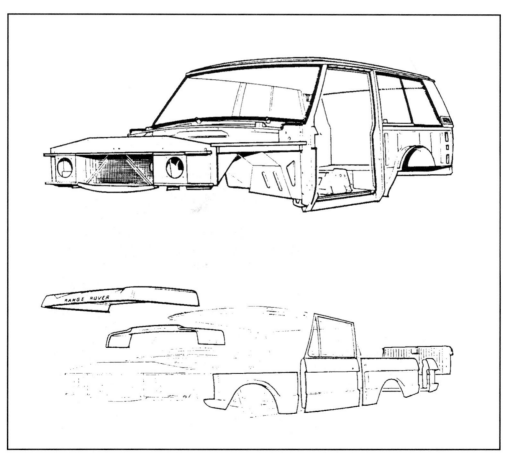

The Range Rover's body consisted of unstressed panels bolted to a steel frame, itself bolted together.

THE RANGE ROVER, 1970 TO 1972

The Range Rover was introduced to the press in June 1970, but examples were not made available to the public until just before the Earls Court Motor Show that October. As a result, only factory-registered vehicles acquired 'H' suffix registrations, and the earliest Range Rovers sold to the public had the 'J' suffix plates introduced in August.

Press reaction to the Range Rover was extremely enthusiastic, but production delays caused many prospective customers to wait several months for their new vehicles, and in fact only just over 2,500 were delivered in the first twelve months. Optional extras were slow to appear through the Rover dealership network, too.

From the beginning, Range Rover marketing linked the vehicle to Rover's luxury saloons rather than to its utilitarian four-wheel drives. Range Rovers shared sales catalogues with the cars, but never with Land-Rovers, although they did have a "by Land-Rover" badge on the tailgate as a reminder of the common heritage. The six paint colours offered were also not dissimilar to those available for Land-Rovers, although the names given to them recalled saloon car practice. Similarly, the PVC upholstery and interior trim materials suggested a Land-Rover

rather than Rover saloon heritage, although the actual comfort levels suggested the opposite. The Range Rover, then, straddled both of the Rover Company's existing markets.

In this delicate balancing act, Rover was taking something of a gamble, and for the first two and a half years of Range Rover sales it concentrated on fine-tuning the vehicle's specification to suit customer demand. In fact, that demand proved to come more from the prestige end of the market than from the utility end and, in due course, the Range Rover created a completely new market niche for luxury four-wheel drive estates.

The very first Range Rovers were in fact quite spartan vehicles, with PVC moulded floor coverings, PVC upholstery, large Land-Rover-like rubber gaiters over the gear levers and three prominent blanking plugs in the dashboard where additional instruments could be fitted. As introduced, they had a lockable limited-slip centre differential, but the limited-slip feature was found to be unnecessary and was discontinued towards the end of 1970. The specification was further "corrected" early in 1971, when a Lockheed brake servo replaced the original Bendix type and, shortly after that, new pistons

An early left-hand-drive Range Rover, dating probably from 1972. Very few survive today in unmodified condition.

In this view of an early Range Rover demonstrating its off-road ability, the early screw-type filler cap can be clearly seen.

The early vehicles had PVC seat facings, integral static safety belts in the front seats, PVC flooring and no outboard seat release handles. Interior trim was not very hard-wearing, and few early Range Rovers still have their original trim.

were fitted to reduce the engine compression ratio from 8.5:1 to 8.25:1.

No optional extras were available before May 1971, when Rover introduced towing and trailer lighting kits, fog and long-range driving lamps, a radio, Sundym tinted glass, a laminated windscreen and a heated rear window. For the 1972 models introduced in October 1971 (by which date the registration suffix had changed to 'K'), there were additional options in the shape of a roof rack, an uprated 18ACR alternator and a split-charge facility for those users who needed a second battery on the vehicle to power additional electrical equipment. Further options introduced during 1972 were a cigarette lighter on the heater surround panel (in January), alternative radios (in April) and - at last - three additional instruments to replace the blanking plugs in the instrument panel. These were an ammeter, an oil pressure gauge and an oil temperature gauge, and all were introduced in April 1972.

For the 1973 model-year, there were further new options and a number of running improvements, but the major modifications were held over until the beginning of the 1973 calendar year. At Earls Court in October 1972, however, the Range Rovers had lower-geared steering (to counter complaints that the steering was heavy), an improved gearchange, a hinged petrol filler cap in place of the earlier screw-on type, and a number of invisible structural improvements. New options were a fuel tank guard plate, front mudflaps, rear seat safety belts, a safety snap-stem interior mirror and a centre PTO, while the number of radio options was reduced to one. The 1973 vehicles attracted 'L' suffix registration numbers.

All Range Rovers are robust vehicles and will take a lot of punishment, but they can also look very scruffy if they have been used hard. As Land Rover Ltd's parts pricing structure is linked to the £35,000 cost of the current Range Rover, it is obvious that restoration of a rough early model will be very expensive. In most cases, it will exceed the cost of buying a good early vehicle. Basket-case early models should therefore be avoided.

Everything is still available to keep one of these early vehicles in running condition, but only if you are prepared to use updated equivalent components in some areas. Parts for the limited-slip centre differential and the original Bendix brake servo have been unavailable for years, for example, so the later type differential or brake servo have to be used complete. Also irreplaceable is the PVC upholstery. For this reason, many early Range Rovers have been updated with later-specification parts.

There are also certain undeniable disadvantages of these early Range Rovers. In original condition, they are much more spartan than later examples (and this is another reason why so many have been updated with later parts). The steering is heavy at parking speeds, even with the lower-geared steering fitted for 1973, and the gearchange is agricultural. Nevertheless, comparing an early Range Rover with a contemporary Land-Rover quickly puts all these deficiencies into perspective!

In other areas, early Range Rovers suffer from very much the same faults as later ones. The main difference is that earlier vehicles are likely to have deteriorated to a greater extent than later ones. What follows is a general guide to the problems you are likely to encounter and the checks you should make when examining an early Range Rover with a view to purchase.

The most obvious areas of deterioration in a Range Rover are all in the body. The steel body frame can rust badly along its "sills" - the lower extremities of the side frame which mount to the chassis outriggers - on the door hinge-posts and around the upper tailgate frame. Rust will also affect the inner rear wheelarches, the front footwell boxes and the front inner wings. Side frame and tailgate frame panels can, theoretically, be unbolted and replaced relatively simply. However, seized bolts and hidden rust tend to make this kind of rebuild of the body frame much more complicated in practice.

The panels bolted to the body frame also deteriorate, to varying degrees. The steel bonnet and lower tailgate are notorious for rusting, the former usually around the plastic "Range Rover" identification letters on its leading edge, and the latter most commonly around the hinged number

plate panel mountings and at its bottom edge. Complete replacement is usually the only viable remedy, and the genuine parts are very expensive, so it is worth noting that "pattern" GRP bonnets and aluminium lower tailgates are available from aftermarket specialists. The upper tailgate around the rear window commonly rusts as well, particularly along the diagonal seams at its lower corners. Very often, this part of the tailgate refuses to shut properly as a result of distortion in the body frame, and Rover actually introduced a rather crude pair of extra clips to hold it shut as a service modification.

The rest of the skin panels are made of aluminium alloy, and so they resist corrosion quite well. However, look for corrosion at the bottom edges of wings and doors, where road salt has accumulated and reacted with the alloy. The alloy panels can also corrode where they touch the steel body frame, and a favourite place for this is where the top edges of the alloy outer front wings are bolted to the steel inner wings. Panels also dent quite easily, and many were quite noticeably rippled from new. Panel fit can be poor, and no early Range Rover should be expected to have even panel gaps all round: with a bolted-together body frame, there was enough room for quite a lot of variation in size between one side of the vehicle and the other!

Still examining the structure of the vehicle, you should now move on to the chassis frame. Bad rusting is uncommon, although it may be present on the side-members above the rear axle (around the bump-rubbers) and on the rear cross-member (between the rear bumper and the fuel tank). The latter can be replaced with a new unit, but sidemember damage will have to be plated. Worth checking, too, is whether there is any chassis damage caused by rough off-road work. Cross-members, in particular, are prone to such damage.

Inside the vehicle, look at the condition of the seats, door trims and floor coverings. As the PVC used for all of them splits and tears quite easily, not many early vehicles are likely to be good in these areas. In the load area, the floor covering suffers, and there might also be dents in the inner wheelarches and rips in the headlining. Most early Range Rovers have by now led a hard life, even if they were pampered by their original owners, so you will be very lucky to find a good interior that is also original.

After this initial series of checks, you should move on to examine the engine. Give it a quick once-over to look for any serious leaks (the rear main bearing seal is a notorious one on early engines, and will drip oil just ahead of the bell-housing), and then move on to a road-test. The V8 is a rugged and robust unit and, when in tip-top condition, it is quiet, smooth and powerful. Its biggest weakness lies in its valve gear, where the hydraulic tappets employed to take up clearances eventually become blocked with sludge. The result then is noisy valve gear and, if this is left too long without attention, the camshaft lobes will also probably wear. If the top end of a Range Rover engine has become noisy, it is best to budget for a change of both camshaft and hydraulic tappets: you should, in any case, never change the camshaft alone or the old tappets will quickly wear it out.

The engine's other main weakness is associated with its aluminium alloy construction. It needs the correct coolant additive (or anti-freeze) all the year round to prevent corrosion of the waterways. An engine which overheats is probably suffering from this condition. Fortunately, however, second-hand engines are both cheap and plentiful. An early Range Rover's transmission is probably one of its least likeable features. Gear selection requires large, slow movements, and there is no known way of eliminating the characteristic whine from the transfer box at speed. There is also a great deal of driveline shunt, thanks to the presence of two gearboxes, two propshafts and three differentials. Serious clunking noises suggest serious wear, though, and gearboxes which jump out of gear should be avoided. Transfer boxes can become starved of oil with expensive results if an internal seal gives way, but unfortunately there is no known way of predicting this problem. Reconditioned gearboxes can, of course, be bought either from Land Rover or from aftermarket specialists.

Lastly, check the condition of the vehicle's running gear. Common problems include tired coil springs (does the vehicle sit all-square?), worn radius arm and Panhard rod bushes (check for free movement) and worn dampers (does the vehicle float or bounce as speed increases?). You should also satisfy yourself that the self-levelling strut is able to raise the rear of a heavily-laden vehicle when it drives off. A worn strut can cause handling problems. Struts are readily available and simple to fit, but expensive.

Steering problems will be most apparent during a road test. Wander or shimmy usually means the ball-joints are worn, and severe kickback over rough surfaces means the damper is unserviceable. Under the vehicle, you should look for corroded or leaking ball swivels, which are the large chromed balls at the ends of the front axle.

Brakes are a Range Rover strong point, although there may be a certain amount of sponginess in the system, and this can be difficult to cure. Check underneath for corroded brake lines and scored discs. On the road, an emergency stop may produce some quite alarming body sway (which is actually a characteristic of all the Range Rovers covered by this book), but the vehicle should pull up squarely. Check the parking brake by seeing if it will hold the vehicle on a slope; these brakes rarely wear out but sometimes need adjustment. Never try to stop a moving vehicle with the handbrake as you will almost certainly damage the transmission.

Between 1973 and 1979, the major elements of the Range Rover's specification changed very little. The reason was quite simply lack of funds. Even though both Land-Rovers and Range Rovers were selling very well indeed, all the profits they made were poured into a corporate pot at British Leyland, and cash was allocated to BL's many divisions according to their needs. As many other BL companies were making losses during this period, very little profit found its way back to Solihull for investment in the future of the Range Rover.

Nevertheless, Rover did what little it could. Some of the 1973 model year changes were held over until January 1973, but from then until the much-improved Range Rovers were introduced in September 1979, small revisions were made at the beginning of every new model year at Motor Show time in October. Sometimes, these changes were hard to detect, but their cumulative effect was to make the 1979-model Range Rover a much more different vehicle from the 1973-model than first appearances would suggest.

The January 1973 changes were the first real improvements - as distinct from "corrections" of the original specification - which were made to the Range Rover. Most of them concerned the interior of the vehicle. The front seat releases were repositioned more accessibly on the outboard edges of the squabs, the transmission tunnel was carpeted (partly to reduce noise levels), a brushed nylon headlining replaced the original vinyl type, and there were new safety-belt catches which met new requirements about single-handed operation. A cigarette lighter could be fitted optionally into the heater surround panel (and in the UK it usually was), and the three circular "blanks" on the instrument panel were now filled by instruments: an oil pressure gauge, an oil temperature gauge, and a voltmeter. In the rear, the load area had been provided with a non-slip floor covering.

These revised vehicles could be recognised from the outside by a wash/wipe system for the tailgate window. Less visible was an uprated (18ACR) alternator. New extra-cost options were a laminated windscreen and Sundym tinted glass, but undoubtedly the most valuable addition to the 1973 models was a power-assisted steering option. As the power steering pump would have been too close to the mechanical fuel pump at the front of the engine, all power-steered Range Rovers were fitted with the electric fuel pump mounted under the body floor which had been standard on export models since the beginning of production.

For the 1974 models (which gained 'M' registration suffixes in Great Britain), Rover made

Although there were changes under the skin at the 1972 Motor Show, the first of the 1973 Range Rovers were hard to distinguish from their forebears. Without the registration number to help, the only way to tell that this is a 1973 model is by the hinged fuel cap.

In January 1973, there were further revisions. This picture shows the outboard seat release levers and the carpeted transmission tunnel. Just visible are the additional instruments in the dashboard.

The rear window wash/wipe and PVC-covered rear quarter-panels were introduced in January 1973, but this is actually a 1974 model.

Under the bonnet. 1974 and later models had a new air intake with thermostatically controlled flap valve.

only small additional changes at the October 1973 Earls Court Show. There were improved mounting arrangements for the tailgate's gas struts, minor alterations to the rear side window frames, and printed instead of engraved plate badges on the scuttle sides. These and black vinyl-covered rear quarter-pillars on the body distinguished the 1974 Range Rovers from earlier models.

Inside, only the relocation of the differential lock warning light on the facia below the instrument binnacle was new for 1974; but there were new options, in the shape of brushed nylon seat facings instead of the PVC type and inertia-reel front seat belts instead of the fixed type. Under the bonnet, nothing had changed except the engine air cleaner,

which now had a thermostatically-controlled intake - an award-winning British Leyland device which also appeared on some Rover and Triumph cars and contributed to faster warm-up and (in theory) to better fuel economy. The electric fuel pump was now standardised on all models, and a vertically-mounted type replaced the earlier horizontal variety.

For 1975 and 'N' registration year, Range Rover customers had to be content with a single change in the paint colour options and the addition of a gear lever gaiter in carpet material in place of the moulded rubber type. Little changed the following year, either. The 1976 ('P' registration) vehicles had improved carpeting on the transmission tunnel, two roof-mounted interior lights instead of one (so that the

Can you tell the difference? This is a 1976 model, fitted with optional foglamps below the front bumper. Note the larger printed plate badges on the scuttle, which had arrived with the 1974 models.

loadspace area was now illuminated), and small modifications to the carburettors. However, the 1976 model-year did see a change in the marketing of Range Rover options. Customers in Britain tended to specify several options together when ordering a new vehicle, and so the most popular of these were combined together into an Option Pack. Probably quite a high proportion of 1976 and later Range Rovers were ordered with this, which consisted of brushed nylon upholstery, front seat head restraints, inertia-reel front seat belts, Sundym tinted glass and power-assisted steering.

Ever since the first fuel crisis in 1973, fuel economy had been an important issue in many Range Rover markets, and it was remarkable that sales of such a thirsty vehicle had not been hit worse than they were. However, Rover took no chances, and introduced two measures in October 1976 on the 1977 model-year ('R' registration) Range Rovers which were designed to improve fuel economy. Taller gearing for the transfer box high ratio was the first of these measures; a more efficient twin-pipe exhaust system was the second. And, of course, a side benefit of the twin-pipe exhaust was the more purposeful-looking dual tail-pipes emerging from below the rear bumper!

Higher compression ratios generally improve fuel economy, so it was surprising to find that the 1978-model Range Rovers introduced in October 1977 actually had a lower compression engine than before. In fact, the change had been dictated by other alterations to the engine needed to meet exhaust emissions regulations in the Australian market, and it was simpler and cheaper for Solihull to make one rather than two types of Range Rover engine: requirements in some overseas markets had already ensured that the parts stocking situation was quite complicated enough! The 1978 ('S' registration) models could also be fitted with door-mounted rear view mirrors, in line with current industry trends, in place of the bonnet-mounted mirrors which had been standard wear since the beginning. For 1979 and 'T' registration year, the only change to the basic Range Rover was that matt black windscreen and tailgate wiper arms replaced the bright type. This, of course, was a deliberate lull before the round of improvements which the newly-created Land Rover Ltd was developing for the 1980 model-year vehicles. However, there was one further enhancement in the autumn of 1978, when the company gave its approval to a Fairey overdrive unit as an extra-cost option which could also be fitted to older vehicles.

BUYING A 1973-1979 RANGE ROVER

At the time of writing, prices for Range Rovers of this era are primarily dependent on condition; the actual age of the vehicle makes very little difference. The main reason for this is that the few changes made to the vehicle's specification between 1973 and 1979 make Range Rovers from this period pretty much of a muchness. Or do they?

First of all, it is not true that the later vehicles were better in all respects than the earlier ones. On paper, the later 8.13:1 compression engines are more powerful and more torquey than the earlier 8.25:1 engines (if this seems illogical, the reason is that the camshaft profile was different). In practice, however, the differences are so small as to be negligible. It is also true that the later transfer box with its taller road gearing makes 1977 and later Range Rovers noticeably less responsive than their predecessors, even if it does save a small amount of fuel.

If fuel consumption is an important consideration, then an overdrive-equipped Range Rover could be what you want. As the overdrive is still available through Land Rover Parts (it is now known as the Superwinch overdrive, as Fairey has changed its name), there is no need to hunt for a vehicle which already has one fitted. You can simply buy one and fit it to a vehicle which has all the other features you want, for the sake of a few hundred pounds. It undoubtedly does improve fuel economy by a small amount, but an overdrive-equipped Range Rover is still unlikely to better 19mpg. In addition, the overdrive adds yet another set of clunks and whines to the already noisy drivetrain. Its advantages, then, are not as clear cut as they might appear at first. Some things really are worth holding out for on Range Rovers of this era, though. Power-assisted steering really is an essential, especially for women drivers. Brushed nylon seats are also well worth having, as they wear so much better than the PVC type and are much more comfortable in extremes of heat and cold. Inertia-reel front seat belts are another "must", as the static type tend to get caught in the door shuts and to prevent the driver from reaching some controls. Is it possible, then, to recommend a Best Buy from among these early Range Rovers? Other things being equal, a 1974, 1975 or 1976 model equipped with the brushed nylon upholstery, inertia-reel belts and power-assisted steering options is likely to prove most satisfactory. Acceleration through the gears is also better on these vehicles than on later ones, because they have the slightly lower transfer box gearing. And, if fuel economy becomes an important factor, it is always possible to add an overdrive while retaining all the existing advantages of the vehicle.

There had still been very little change by the time this 1978 model was built. Door mirrors were new for 1978. Note the foglamps, still optional but now Lucas Square 8s and fitted with protective covers.

THE RANGE ROVER, 1980 TO 1981

In July 1978, Land Rover Ltd was established as a separate operating company within the British Leyland empire. The following month, the company announced that it had been granted £280 million to fund a two-stage plan, scheduled for completion in 1984. This would both expand its production capacity and see the introduction of new models. As far as the Range Rover was concerned (although this was not announced at the time), the two stages would consist of a face-lift and a 50% increase in production, followed by a further increase in production and the introduction of a series of major specification improvements.

The first effects on Range Rovers of the new investment scheme were seen in September 1979. There were three bright new paint options for the 1980-model Range Rovers announced that month, which also had black polyester-coated bumpers in place of the aluminium-finish originals, decal badges on bonnet and tailgate (to help cut down on rusting caused by the holes for the earlier separate letters), and repeater flashers on the front wings. The plate badges had also gone from the scuttle sides and there were new tail-lights incorporating fog-guard lamps. These improved Range Rovers had 'V' registration suffixes in Great Britain.

Inside the 1980 models, the brushed nylon seats with PVC headrests and inertia-reel safety belts at

This 1980 Range Rover clearly shows many of the features which were new for that season's models. Note the black bumper, decal bonnet badge, wing mounted indicator repeater lamp and the absence of scuttle badges. Even the tyres are different, although the change was not total: the factory was simply buying in from two suppliers instead of one

In this rear view of the same vehicle can be seen the new tail-lamps, with a high intensity fog guard lamp built in and a smaller reversing lamp sector. Note also the twin tailpipe, first seen on 1977 models.

Whereas 1980 models had one-piece head restraints on the front seats, the 1981 Range Rovers came with detachable head restraint cushions.

the front were now standard, and there was a new four-spoke steering wheel. Warning lamps for the rear fog guard lamps and for brake vacuum loss were added to the facia and Sundym glass was standardised. All vehicles were now fitted with door mirrors, halogen headlamps and a higher-output (25ACR) alternator, and there was a new and still taller high ratio in the transfer box to aid fuel economy. And, to meet a demand which had been catered for by various aftermarket specialists, factory-fitted air conditioning became optional, complete with a redesigned dashboard incorporating additional outlet vents.

An inevitable side-effect of the improved specification for the 1980 model-year was an increase in showroom prices, and Land Rover feared that this might deter fleet users like the Police, who had no need of the luxury items on the latest models. In order to retain a fleet market for the Range Rover, Land Rover therefore introduced a low-specification model called the Fleet Line, which was kept cheaper

than the standard vehicle by its use of pleated Ambla leathercloth upholstery, its retention of the original PVC flooring and its lack of power steering.

The 1980 models' improvements were followed up by further changes for the 1981 season, although these were fewer in number and less far-reaching. Most important from many points of view was that the Range Rover's chassis was now galvanised and electrophoretically corrosion-proofed before being painted in its familiar black enamel. A narrower gearchange gate made some improvement to the change quality. More noticeable than either of these, however, was the improved interior trim. The upholstery was now in brushed velour instead of brushed nylon, in a slightly darker colour than before which was known as Bronze. Front seat head restraints were covered in velour instead of PVC and had detachable cushions. There were removable carpets front and rear over rubber flooring, carpet-type trim instead of PVC on the door bottoms, and carpet on the leading edges of the rear wheel arches.

BUYING A 1980-1981 RANGE ROVER

The 1980-1981 model Range Rovers - Fleet Line versions apart - were very much more refined vehicles than their predecessors. Gear whine was still present in abundance, driveline shunt had not been eliminated, and build quality was no better than before; but the little improvements did show. Unless there are good reasons for buying an earlier Range Rover, therefore, these models are an all-round better bet.

All these vehicles have power steering; all have heated rear windows and rear wash/wipe systems; all have door mirrors and all have cloth upholstery. Their halogen headlamps are much more powerful than the earlier sealed-beam type, and the raised transfer gearing gives optimum fuel economy, albeit at the expense of acceleration through the gears. In this case, newer is also better. The 1981-season brushed velour upholstery and fuller carpeting do help to make the vehicles appear more luxurious, and make the 1981 models an even better buy than the 1980s. Prices, as with the earlier models, are more dependent on condition than on age.

Both bonnet and lower tailgate are less prone to rusting than on earlier examples because they have no piercings for the badging letters. Tailgates still do rust, though, as they still have the hinged number plate fitting which was the principal source of the trouble.

On Fleet Line models, the lack of power steering is a disadvantage and is certainly a bargaining point when considering a purchase. The Ambla upholstery in these vehicles, however, is much more hard-wearing than the earlier PVC type and need not be a deterrent to purchase if it is in good condition.

1980 official press photograph.

THE RANGE ROVER MONTEVERDI

Almost as soon as finance became available for Range Rover development in 1978, work seems to have started on a four-door body. In fact, Rover had produced a first four-door Range Rover prototype as long ago as 1971, but there had then been insufficient funds to put it into production. While Solihull was preparing its revitalised version for production, however, it was approached by the Swiss specialist car manufacturer Peter Monteverdi, who was seeking the company's agreement to honour its standard warranty on a four-door luxury conversion he had just developed.

Land Rover Ltd saw in the Monteverdi vehicle an opportunity to blaze a trail for its own four-door model, and to test the market for more luxuriously equipped Range Rovers. So it agreed to honour its standard warranty on the Monteverdi four-door vehicle, and at the same time offered to promote the vehicle and sell it through selected Land Rover dealerships as an extension of its own range. Monteverdi agreed to the deal, and the Range Rover Monteverdi was first shown in public at the Geneva Motor Show in March 1980. The UK launch was at Earls Court that October.

Although the original plan was for Monteverdi to convert about 300 vehicles a year, in fact only 50 were ever made. Of these, 35 were sold through U.K. dealers and 15 were sold in Europe. The details are far from clear, but it looks as if Land Rover Ltd brought forward plans to launch its own four-door model and, when this was announced in July 1981, Monteverdi production was halted. Not all the Monteverdis had been sold by the time the factory four-door model appeared, and this must have hindered sales because the Monteverdi was very much the more expensive vehicle. Some examples were not put on the road until well into 1982.

The Monteverdi vehicles were converted in Switzerland from fully-built two-door Range Rovers, which were shipped from Solihull finished in white primer. The body conversion provided them with shortened front doors and an extra pair of rear doors. It is easily distinguishable from the factory's own four-door by the curved trailing edge to the rear door and by the full-height quarter-window in the front door. Many Monteverdis, though not all, also wore distinctive badging on the grille, tailgate and scuttle sides, and some non-factory paint finishes were offered. Air conditioning was standard (it was fitted on the production line at Solihull before the vehicles were shipped), and Monteverdis also had a luxuriously trimmed interior. Cloth upholstery was standard and pleated leather an option, and either could be ordered in a choice of beige, black or tan at a time when the factory offered only Bronze cloth trim. The vehicles had a fully-carpeted rear load area, a unique lidded storage box on the transmission tunnel, and a neat fairing over the instrument binnacle which made it look better integrated with the dashboard.

In practice, the Monteverdi seems to have been very much a custom-built vehicle, and probably no two were exactly alike. Some, for example, were finished in colours not offered in the sales catalogue for the model. Monteverdi also made at least one turbocharged vehicle, which he displayed at the Geneva Motor Show in March 1981, but that seems to have been something of a last-ditch attempt to gather sales in the face of the imminent arrival of the factory four-door. In fact, Monteverdi did go on to make a few luxury conversions for private customers using the factory's own four-door body and - although the exercise came to nothing - was asked to produce a Range Rover design study for Land Rover Ltd in late 1981 or early 1982.

The Monteverdi conversion is most easily recognisable from the side, when the curved rear door cutout and full-height front quarter window are visible.

This interior view of the Monteverdi shows the leather seats, pleated door trim panels and the storage box on the transmission tunnel. This example hs also been fitted with an overdrive (note the additional lever alongside the storage box) and - in recent years - a diesel engine.

The instrument binnacle cowl was also unique to the Monteverdi four-door model.

BUYING A MONTEVERDI

The real problem with buying a Monteverdi is finding one for sale. As there are fewer than three dozen examples in the UK, it would be unwise to pass one up if you really want one of these rare beasts. However, you should be wary of any examples offered which need major repair work, for the simple reason that many parts are no longer available from Land Rover Ltd. Doors, rear wings, side glass, sill finishers, upholstery and trim are all unique to the model, and many of them have been unavailable for years: Land Rover Ltd no longer stocks them and the Monteverdi company closed in 1988. Major repair work would therefore demand custom-built panels, which would be very costly indeed.

The metal used in the custom-built parts is said to be of poor quality, and to be prone to corrosion. Rear wheelarch panels and rear floor sections can be badly affected. On the brighter side, however, the Monteverdi's mechanical specification is exactly the same as for a contemporary factory-built Range Rover. This means that everyday running spares will not prove problematical.

The Monteverdi undeniably has considerable attractions for the Range Rover enthusiast. It is rare and it is different, and those factors might be enough to risk the purchase of a vehicle which could be difficult to repair if it is damaged in an accident. For most would-be Range Rover owners, though, it is one to avoid. For this reason, prices are likely to be generally similar to those for early (and much less well-equipped) factory four-door Range Rovers.

It probably goes without saying that to modify a Monteverdi today would be a mistake. One day, these vehicles are going to be extremely rare, and it would be a pity if none remained in original condition as examples of what the first factory-approved four-door Range Rovers were like. That said, of course, it is by no means easy to establish exactly what the specification of any given Monteverdi would have been when it was new. As they were more or less custom-built, the only way of establishing the original specification would be from documents relating to the ordering, build, or initial sale of the vehicle.

Monteverdi's conversions had special badging....

... but not all the badges were the same. The alloy wheels and the arch extensions on this example were not standard but could have been fitted from new.

RANGE ROVER IN VOGUE, 1981

The Monteverdi four-door model had been Land Rover Ltd's first test of the market for a more expensive Range Rover, but it was a test which was to be cut short when the company's own four-door model was introduced in summer 1981. Perhaps, then, Land Rover's marketing people considered that they needed further evidence of how a luxury Range Rover would sell before they could wholeheartedly endorse the move up-market which was already in the planning stages for the vehicle.

One way or another, the company this time made contact with Wood and Pickett of London, who had been the leading builders of luxury Range Rover conversions for Middle Eastern markets during the 1970s. Late in 1980, a prototype two-door model with a limited amount of luxury equipment was built as a joint effort between Land Rover's own stylists and Wood and Pickett. The Land Rover marketing people then arranged a link-up with the high fashion magazine *Vogue*. The prototype travelled to Biarritz with the magazine's photographers and was used as a backdrop in photographs of the 1981 Lancôme and Jaeger fashion collections.

The aim was simple: exposing the vehicle in Vogue magazine publicised it in exactly those social circles in which Land Rover wanted to sell the more up-market Range Rovers it was planning, and the link-up with high fashion collections reinforced the

image of exclusivity already associated with the Range Rover. It was a marketing coup in more ways than one, for Land Rover also agreed to call the planned limited-edition run of these vehicles the Range Rover In Vogue. It was perhaps a clumsy name - and was soon familiarly shortened to Range Rover Vogue - but it certainly achieved its aim.

The In Vogue model had not in fact been announced when it appeared in Vogue magazine, and the magazine feature made no special reference to it. However, the sales catalogue for the vehicle reproduced many of the pictures from the magazine and thus emphasised the link between the two. Exclusivity was maintained by making the In Vogue a limited edition of 1,000 vehicles, all with right hand drive and all for the UK market.

The Range Rover In Vogue was made available from February 1981 and was instantly distinguishable from the ordinary two-door model by its pale metallic blue paint and broad coach lines in two contrasting shades of grey. Although the prototype pictured in Vogue magazine had also had three-spoke alloy wheels of a striking new design, these would not actually become available until later in 1981, and it is unlikely that any of the 1,000 production models were fitted with them from new. Instead, production In Vogue models had a slightly modified pressed-steel wheel with an enlarged centre

In this picture the only indication that this is a 1981 In Vogue special is the twin coachline on the body-sides. In the metal, the striking metallic blue paint is an immediate recognition feature

cut-out into which were fitted black rubber inserts bearing the Range Rover name.

Inside the In Vogue, the standard cloth trim remained, although the head restraints on the front seats came with detachable cushions like those seen in the Monteverdi. The in-dash air conditioning system was also standard, and there was a stereo radio/cassette unit with four speakers. Wood and Pickett's contribution had been polished walnut door cappings, a lidded storage box between the front seats (added because the standard glove-box could not be fitted with air conditioning), and map pockets on the seat backs. In addition, they had provided full carpeting for the load area, a matching spare wheel cover and a picnic hamper which fitted neatly behind the right-hand wheelarch. Lastly, there was a stainless steel capping on the tailgate to prevent

damage when loading or unloading.

The In Vogue was also the first production Range Rover to have the new high-compression engine which would not become standard on other models until autumn 1981. The point of this was to improve fuel economy at a time when the issue was a major marketing consideration as a result of the 1979 fuel crisis. So it was that the Range Rover engine's compression ratio had been raised to 9.35:1 by using the pistons from its Rover 3500 saloon equivalent. In addition, a stiffened cylinder block on these engines helped to reduce noise levels, and a new distributor incorporated long-life sliding contact points. Further gains in fuel economy were achieved from taller gearing, achieved by raising the high ratio in the transfer box; low ratio, however, remained unchanged.

1981 season Range Rover in Vogue special edition, showing polished wooden door cappings.

BUYING A RANGE ROVER IN VOGUE

Even though 1,000 In Vogue Range Rovers were built, they are not easy to find. If you are determined to have one of these vehicles, then, you might have to spend a long time looking. Beware of lookalikes - two-door Range Rovers which were resprayed in Vogue Blue and dressed up to look like the In Vogue model. However, the cost of fitting all the In Vogue parts was enough to deter owners from building complete replicas, and non-authentic vehicles will almost certainly lack some of the In Vogue's characteristic features. Real In Vogue models will have W- or X-suffix registrations, unless they have been registered with a "personal" plate.

When buying an In Vogue, probably the most important thing to check is whether all the items unique to the vehicle are intact. The wooden door cappings, console-mounted storage box and picnic hamper can be replaced through Land Rover dealers in theory, but there must come a time when stocks of these low-volume parts will be exhausted.

On the mechanical side, an In Vogue is identical to the later 1982-model two-door Range Rover. It therefore presents no special problems of maintenance or ownership. As many first owners of these vehicles bought them for prestige reasons rather than as workhorses, it is also likely that In Vogue models will have survived in rather better condition than many of their contemporaries. But this need not be the case: subsequent owners might not have looked after the vehicle so carefully.

As far as prices are concerned, owners are likely to expect to realise rather more for these limited-edition vehicles than they might get for a standard two-door Range Rover of the same age. In support of that argument, it is true that the vehicles are much better equipped than the standard models. However, it is also true that an In Vogue has only two doors and a four-speed gearbox, both of which argue against a high purchase price!

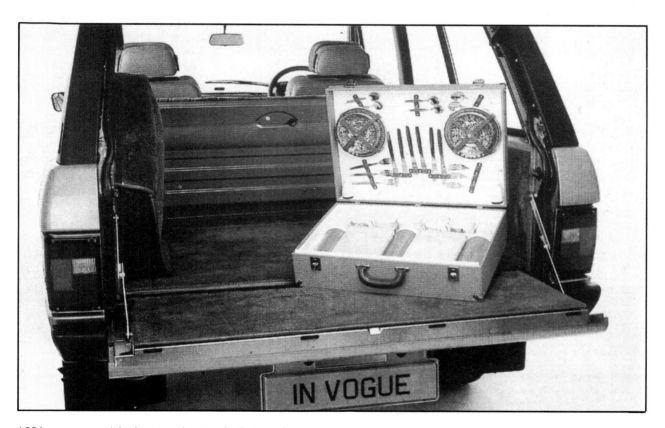

1981 season model, showing the standard picnic hamper.

TWO-DOOR AND FOUR-DOOR RANGE ROVERS, 1982

The 1982 model Range Rovers were announced in July 1981 and the most important piece of news was that, at last, Land Rover had introduced its own four-door model. The Monteverdi, now redundant, disappeared from the company's sales catalogues; but the original two-door body remained available alongside the new four-door.

Land Rover had put a lot of effort into getting the vehicle to look right. From the side, it was undoubtedly neater than Monteverdi's creation, thanks to rear doors which closed over the wheelarch and thus eliminated the untidy shut-line of the Swiss-built vehicles, and to a smaller front quarter-light which made the front door look better proportioned. Blacked-out window pillars all round also helped to slim the lines. Like the Monteverdi, however, the factory-built four-door had Morris Marina door handles instead of the edge pulls used on two-door models.

There had been careful attention inside, as well. The four-door body boasted redesigned door trims, this time covering all the metalwork and adding to the luxurious ambience, and the rear seat had been moved back by three inches to give extra legroom. The central storage box first seen on the 1981 In Vogue was a standard fitting, which was in keeping with the general improvements in the Range Rover's equipment levels, but it was surprising to find that, despite the presence of a strong centre door pillar, the front seat safety belts were still mounted integrally with the seats themselves. Options for the four-door models only were a pair of metallic paint finishes (the first on a Range Rover), electric window lifts, polished rosewood veneer door cappings and loadspace carpeting. All four items could be had together in an Option Pack, which also included an option which was available for the two-door models: a set of stylish polished alloy three-spoke wheels with black rubber centre badges like those on 1981's In Vogue.

When alloy wheels were not specified, 1982 model Range Rovers had the familiar five-spoke pressed steel type. Both two-door and four-door models also incorporated a series of enhancements, all designed to improve their appeal in the luxury market. They had new windscreen wash/wipe controls, which gave two wiper speeds, a flick-wipe facility, an intermittent wipe cycle and a linked wash-and-wipe cycle. They also had new sun visors with a vanity mirror on the passenger's side and a ticket pocket on the driver's, a courtesy lamp delay, map pockets behind the front seats, and carpet material instead of black plastic covering the spare wheel and tool kit in the rear. All except the Fleet Line two-door models also had twin underbonnet lamps and were factory-fitted with a radio aerial, front door speakers, and all the necessary wiring for a radio of the customer's choice. Two-door Range Rovers with the optional air conditioning had the 1981 In Vogue's central storage box, and this could also be had to special order on other two-door models.

Last but not least, all the 1982 model Range Rovers had the high-compression engine and taller transfer gearing previewed earlier in the year on the In Vogue limited edition. The original argument for a low-compression engine still held good, of course, and so the earlier engine remained available for some overseas markets. But most Range Rovers were being sold in the civilised world, and the Land Rover view was that the high-compression engine would improve sales. Maximum torque remained almost unchanged in the new engine, with the result that the Range Rover lost none of its accelerative ability or its off-road prowess. Maximum power was down by 7bhp, but the power peak was reached at 4,000rpm instead of 5,000rpm, with the result that the engine was both quieter and more economical at high speeds. The taller transfer gearing of course simply enhanced both these qualities.

The very early four-speed, four-door models could be recognised easily by the keylock in the door panel below the handle.

The dashboard of the early four-door Range Rover, fitted in this case with the optional air conditioning, for which the vents can be seen in the facia rail. The door trims were much plainer than in the Monteverdi conversions.

Right: Even though the rear seat had been moved back to give more legroom, the load area on the four-door Range Rover was simply enormous. Note the carpet material covering the spare wheel and the tool storage panel.

With the 1982 Range Rovers, the popularity of the two-door model began to decline. The four-door was - and is - so much more practical as a passenger-carrying vehicle that two-doors soon became the exception rather than the rule. There are relatively few X-registered two-door models around in Great Britain.

The 1982 models are undoubtedly more refined than their predecessors, thanks to the high-compression engine and taller transfer gearing. But they suffer from transmission backlash and gear whine in just the same way as all four-speed models. The extra weight of the four-door models also means that the improvements in fuel economy which the new drivetrain offers on paper are seldom realised in practice.

The 1982 Range Rovers also have some problem areas which earlier models do not. The headlining on four-door models is more prone than that on two-doors to sagging at the join between the two pieces - perhaps because the opening and closing of the rear doors places additional strain on its fixings. The electric window lifts can become irritatingly slow in operation, and the smart alloy wheels can corrode. Once this has happened, they are hard to refurbish - and they are expensive to replace. As far as the four-door bodies are concerned, there is an additional area to examine for rust, on the forward edge of the rear wheelarch, where it is covered by the rear door. By way of compensation, however, the lighter doors mean that four-doors do not generally suffer from the door dropping problems associated with two-door models.

An irritating weakness of the four-door models are the plastic press studs which hold the two-piece headlining in place. This picture shows the headlining as it should be, but many hang down in the centre.

The polished alloy wheel option was first seen on 1982-model Range Rovers. The black centre bung is embossed with the Range Rover name.

THE 1983 RANGE ROVERS

The 1980s saw a steady upgrading of the Range Rover, with major improvements being introduced every year. For 1980, the basic two-doors had been refined; for 1981, interior trim had been improved and the high-compression engine had arrived; for 1982, the four-door body had been introduced; and for 1983, the major introduction was an automatic transmission option.

To those who still thought of the Range Rover as a sort of super-Land Rover, the whole idea of an automatic transmission seemed strange. But there had been a steady demand for automatic transmission conversions in the luxury market for which the custom-builders catered, and most of the big American four-wheel drive estates had had automatic transmission for years. As Land Rover's (unpublicised) intention was to take the Range Rover into the American market for which it had always been intended as soon as possible, an automatic option was an essential development.

So, in August 1982, Land Rover announced that both two- and four-door Range Rovers for the 1983 model-year would be available with a three-speed American Chrysler Torqueflite A727 automatic transmission as an alternative to the standard four-speed manual. Bolted to this was a new transfer box designed and built by Land Rover, and called the LT230R. This had slightly taller gearing than the integral transfer box of the manual Range Rovers, in order to offset fuel eonomy losses through the automatic transmission. It also had a simpler control system, in which the centre differential lock was combined with the ratio change lever.

Automatic Range Rovers had a neat console arrangement around the transmission levers, incorporating a coin tray and two ashtrays. They also had a transmission oil temperature warning lamp on the dashboard, as the A727 could overheat in extreme conditions; for the same reason, automatic models had a transmission oil cooler ahead of the radiator. To accommodate the automatic transmission and new transfer box, the exhaust system had been modified, and the revised type was fitted to all 1983 Range Rovers; from behind, it could be distinguished by a new tailpipe with the pipe ends burred-over instead of cut away at an angle. All 1983 models also came with overriders at the ends of the front bumper, a coin tray instead of the radio speaker grille on the dashboard, a leather-covered steering wheel and ISO-standard column switchgear (in which the indicators were now on the left and the wash-wipe controls on the right). Other 1983 improvements were unique to the four-door models, however. These were already selling so well that further development of the two-door Range Rover as a model in its own right had effectively been abandoned.

The additional improvements for the 1983 four-doors were all options. There were two more metallic paint colours, and a series of upgrades for the interior. These were a rear centre armrest, twin rear head restraints, and armrests on the inboard edges of the front seats. To give these new items and the automatic transmission maximum exposure, Land Rover put them all into a new special-edition model.

The main news for 1983 was that an automatic transmission was now available. This is the dashboard of an early automatic Range Rover. Note the rectangular tops to the main and transfer gear selector levers, and the coin tray which replaced the radio speaker grille in the centre of the dash of the 1983 models.

RANGE ROVER AUTOMATIC IN VOGUE SPECIAL EDITION, 1983

For the new special-edition Range Rover, Land Rover revived the In Vogue name, although there was no link-up this time with Vogue magazine. The new special-edition model was exactly that, and not a limited edition like the earlier two-door In Vogue. For that reason, it is impossible to say exactly how many were built: quite possibly, the majority of 1983-model four-door automatics for the home market were finished as In Vogue Special Editions.

The 1983 In Vogue came with everything which was new for 1983: automatic transmission, armrests and rear head restraints, and Nevada Gold or Sierra Silver metallic paint. Gold models had a broad coachline in two-tone brown, while Silver vehicles had a similar one in two-tone grey. All the In Vogues had three-spoke alloy wheels, distinguished from those optional elsewhere by their grey enamelled finish. In addition, there were elegant inlaid wood door cappings, and a cool box in the loadspace. Air conditioning, however, was optional rather than standard as on the earlier two-door In Vogue models.

Left: The wooden door cappings and adjustable armrests were options on the 1983 models, on which front safety harnesses were still integral with the seats.

Below: Distinguishing features of the 1983 model Automatic In Vogue were metallic paintwork, coachlines on the flanks and shaded alloy wheels. The front bumper overriders seen on this example were standard on all models for 1983

BUYING A 1983 RANGE ROVER

Most Range Rovers sold in Great Britain during the 1983 model-year were four-door models; not many two-doors were registered with that year's Y-suffix plates, except for Fleet Lines ordered by Police Forces and other fleet users. Very few of those two-doors had the new automatic transmission.

Although the three-speed automatic transmission makes a Range Rover more relaxing to drive than the four-speed manual gearbox, it does have some disadvantages. One of these is that it takes the edge off acceleration; another is that it does nothing for fuel consumption. These shortcomings were thrown into sharp relief in October 1985, when Land Rover replaced the Chrysler three-speed automatic by a much more modern ZF four-speed type. As a result, the three-speed automatic is not generally considered to be a desirable option. In fact, it is by no means a bad gearbox, and is both tough and reliable in service.

Of the other 1983 introductions, the additional armrests and rear head restraints do make the Range Rover's passenger cabin that little bit more luxurious, and are worth looking for if luxury is important to you. All of them are, of course, standard on the In Vogue Special Edition Range Rovers, which are quite desirable vehicles if you are prepared to live with the three-speed automatic transmission and the rather garish paint schemes. Not for nothing did Land Rover abandon Nevada Gold and Sierra Silver after only three seasons! One particular drawback of these special edition models is their inlaid wood door cappings. When in pristine condition, these look beautiful, but if damaged, they are hard to repair and make the interior look very down-at-heel.

Contrary to many people's expectations, electric window lifts and air conditioning were not standard on the 1983 In Vogue models. Some have them, but others do not. And it is worth checking, if you are offered one of these models for sale, that it still has the proper accessory cool box in the rear.

Land Rover had another major change lined up for the 1984-model Range Rovers: the introduction of a five-speed manual gearbox in place of the four-speed type used since production had begun. The new LT77 gearbox had in fact been in production for several years and had appeared in cars from Rover, Jaguar and Triumph, but this was its first application to a four-wheel drive vehicle. It was paired with a version of the LT230R transfer box introduced a year earlier on the automatic-transmission Range Rovers.

The five-speed gearbox was available on both two-door and four-door Range Rovers. The long, wand-like, gearlever which came with it was much like that on the superseded four-speed models, but the five-speed Range Rovers did have a new centre console panel which was broadly similar to the type introduced on the automatic versions a year earlier. Both the main and transfer gear levers (the latter now incorporating the differential lock) were provided with neat gaiters, and the handbrake lever had a ribbed cover. All 1984 model Range Rovers also had a new torsion bar balancing system to make the heavy lower tailgate easier to open and close, and a hydraulic jack replaced the screw type in the tool kit behind the right-hand rear wheel arch. Both changes were clearly designed to make the Range Rover simpler to use, particularly for women drivers.

Four-door models were now given the added refinement of a central locking system, and their front door keylocks were now fitted in the door handles themselves instead of below them, as on earlier vehicles. Two-doors for 1984 had blacked-out window pillars like their four-door counterparts for the first time. As far as Great Britain was concerned, however, this change affected only Fleet Line models, as two-door sales to private customers had effectively ceased.

The Option Pack arrangement was also rationalised for 1984, and three were now offered - but for the four-door models only. In each case, the individual items were available separately, but the Option Packs offered substantial savings when the cost of the individual items they contained was added up. Option Pack C provided front and rear armrests, rear head restraints, wooden door cappings and carpet for the loadspace and lower tailgate platform. Option Pack B added alloy wheels and metallic paint to this selection, and Option Pack A added air conditioning to the contents of Option Pack B.

The success of the 1981 and 1983 In Vogue models prompted Land Rover to introduce a third In Vogue model to promote the 1984 models and this, once again, bore the In Vogue name.

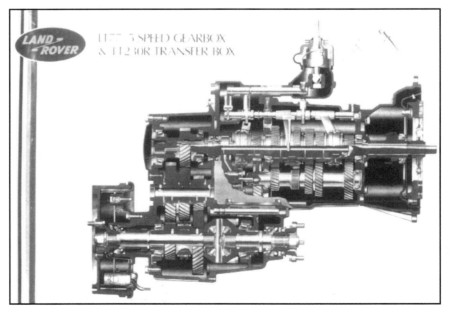

A cutaway diagram of the five-speed LT77 gearbox and its accompanying LT230R transfer box.

With the 1984 models came the five-speed manual gearbox. The long, wand-like gear lever was much the same as on the superseded four-speed models, but the differential lock was now operated through the transfer lever, as on the automatic models. Note also the new, ribbed cover for the handbrake lever. This is an air-conditioned model, as the four dashboard vents make clear.

Outboard armrests for the rear seats became optional on 1984 models. The armrests, rear head restraints and wooden door cappings were all part of Option Pack C, fitted to the vehicle pictured. The black plastic "flower pot" on the D-pillar is a keep for the buckle of the optional rear seat belts, which were not fitted in this case.

RANGE ROVER IN VOGUE, 1984

The 1984 model In Vogue was announced in August 1983, one month later than the 1984 season's five-speed Range Rovers, and was promoted in conjunction with the Daks autumn fashion collection at Simpson's in London's Piccadilly. Once again it was a limited edition model, of which only 325 were made available for the UK market. It had the four-door body, and came with a choice of five-speed manual or three-speed automatic transmissions. Together with 1984's only new colour - Derwent Blue metallic - it had the usual Vogue twin broad coachlines on the body sides and the same grey-enamelled three-spoke alloy wheels as the 1983 Automatic In Vogue Special Edition.

Other special features were walnut veneer door cappings, front and rear armrests and rear head restraints, rear seat belts, a black tailgate capping, a cool box and a picnic hamper in the rear loadspace, and a digital radio/cassette unit with four speakers.

BUYING A 1984 RANGE ROVER

The 1984-model Range Rovers, most of which acquired A-suffix registration numbers in Great Britain, have some worthwhile improvements over their predecessors. The biggest of these is undoubtedly the new five-speed manual gearbox, which does away with much of the transmission shunt which had affected the four-speed models. As the fifth gear is an overdrive, it also reduces engine noise and fuel consumption at cruising speeds. There is also less gear whine from the LT230R transfer box than from the integral transfer box of the four-speed transmission. Gear ratios are better spaced for road work than on the four-speed models, and shift quality is also much improved, but the long gear lever still makes rapid gear selection difficult.

Other real benefits of the 1984 models are the lightened tailgate operation and the central locking on four-door vehicles. This, however, operates only from the driver's door and does not cover the upper tailgate: the multi-point central locking which remedied both of these deficiencies was not introduced until several years later. Large numbers of the four-door Range Rovers sold on the home market during the 1984 model year were ordered with one of the Option Packs, a fact which encouraged Land Rover in its intention to push the Range Rover further up-market. Probably a majority of 1984 four-door models had at least the intermediate pack, which brought with it alloy wheels, metallic paint, armrests and rear head restraints, wooden door cappings and a carpeted rear loadspace.

So many 1984 Range Rovers were highly specified from new that the In Vogue limited-edition models stand out very little. Prices are therefore unlikely to be higher than those for the "ordinary" vehicles. The only disadvantage of the In Vogue models is the vulnerability of the veneered door cappings. Otherwise, and as with earlier In Vogue models, you should check that all the special equipment is still intact when viewing one of these vehicles for sale. Owners often retain the picnic hampers and cool boxes when they sell the vehicles on!

THE 1985 RANGE ROVERS

The 1985 model-year was the last one in which all Range Rovers would have the carburetted 3.5-litre engine, and it was also one which introduced several major improvements which put the four-door Range Rover firmly into the luxury car class. Although two-door Fleet Line models continued to be built for fleet users like Police Forces, and two-door models continued to be available for certain overseas markets, very few private customers indeed took delivery of two-door models with B-suffix registrations in Great Britain.

The 1985-model Range Rovers were announced in June 1984. Immediate recognition points were the new decal badges on bonnet and tailgate, which now had brown or silver letters instead of the black type edged with white; and, on the four-door models, the front quarter-light had been deleted altogether to tidy up the side view and remove one source of wind-noise at speed. Both two-door and four-door models also had new door mirrors in black plastic, mounted to the lower leading edge of the window frame instead of to the door panel.

The biggest changes for the 1985 models had been made inside the passenger compartment. A new heater with a 50% greater output and controls illuminated from above fed new ducting which took air to the rear footwells and to side window demister vents at the ends of the dashboard. The dashboard itself had been extensively redesigned, with a switchgear panel beside the heater controls, matched by the lid of the new fusebox on the other side. Above this centre section were a pair of multi-directional air vents flanking a new quartz clock.

There was a grab handle for the passenger on the dash, and an open parcel shelf took the place of the earlier glove box - except, that is, when air conditioning was fitted, when the area was blanked off. Most noticeable of all, perhaps, was a new instrument binnacle, much larger than before, and containing a quadrant-style speedometer and rev counter. Between these was a bank of warning lights, and the water temperature and fuel gauges were set into the rev counter. There were revisions to the column switches, too, to cope with the new

intermittent wipe function for the tailgate wiper.

The seats had also been altered considerably. The standard upholstery was now Bronze Check cloth, and the seats themselves had height adjustment and reclining backrests for the first time. Redesigned headrests complemented the new upholstery and there were new door trims with high-mounted speakers in the front pair on four-door models. When fitted with wooden door cappings, these trims also had a matching wooden fillet on their closing pulls. On four-door models, the front safety belts were no longer integral with the seats but were instead mounted to the centre pillar, where their top mountings were adjustable for height.

The 1985 models also brought sundry other improvements: electronic ignition, a weather strip on the rear bumper, black tailgate capping (as seen on the 1984 In Vogue), revised upper tailgate struts with an over-centre action, an improved wiring harness and a pair of new paint colours. There were new options, too, but these and all the other new features were found together as standard on the new Vogue model, which was now a regular production option.

The Vogue - no longer an In Vogue - was readily distinguished by its grey enamelled three-spoke alloy wheels, bodyside tapes, and luxurious silver-grey velour upholstery. Door trims and headlining were of course also finished in grey to match, and these models were the first factory built examples ever to have an interior in any colour other than brown. The rear headlining above the tailgate also incorporated a pair of extra stereo speakers, which feature was optional on ordinary four-door models. Other 1985 options fitted as standard to the Vogue models were headlamp washers mounted in the front bumper, a rigid folding cover for the rear loadspace, wooden door cappings and fillets, and door mirrors with electric demisting and adjustment.

One option introduced for 1985 and not fitted to the Vogue did not prove popular, however: customers seem not to have thought very highly of the rather garish decal side panel which could be added just below the window line.

The 1985 Vogues were the first Range Rovers to have grey upholstery material.

The 1985 models were distinguished by a revised dashboard, with minor switchgear alongside the heater panel, a centrally mounted clock, and a completely new instrument binnacle.

Height adjustable front seats also arrived on 1985 models, and with them came a new Bronze Check upholstery. The seat belt upper mountings were now mounted to the B/C pillars on height-adjustable brackets.

For 1985 the Vogue became a catalogued model. The 1985 Vogues can be readily recognised by their bodyside tapes, grey-enamelled alloy wheels and headlamp washer jets on the bumper. All 1985 models shared the new front door glasses without quarter-lights, the neatly redesigned door mirrors and the solid lettering for the decal badges.

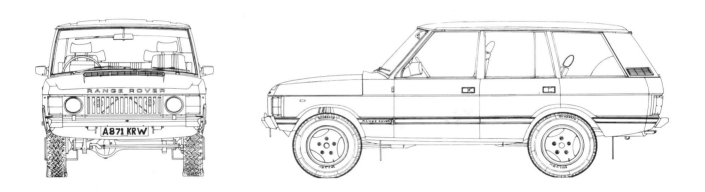

1984 RANGE ROVER 4 DOOR VOGUE

© Trevor N Alder 1986

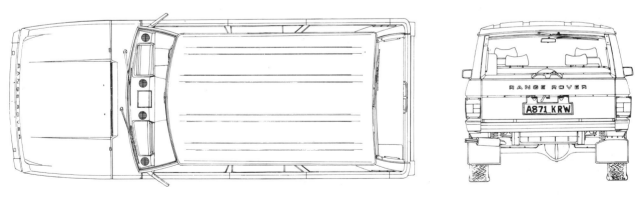

Copies of this and other Range Rover drawings on A3 card are available from T. N. Alder on 0473 251906.

BUYING A 1985 RANGE ROVER

The 1985 season models were tremendously successful and broke all sales records for the Range Rover. The new Vogue model accounted for over 80% of sales in the UK, which meant that there were relatively few ordinary four-door models, and two-doors were all but extinct on the home market, although they continued to find buyers overseas. In the UK, the automatic transmission also proved popular, and some 40% of 1985 models had it.

There is no doubt that the improved interiors of the 1985 Range Rovers make these into proper luxury conveyances. The seats are more comfortable than earlier types as well as being fully adjustable, and the new dashboard gives a much more car-like feel to the vehicle. However, the gearchange on manual models is still rather vague, and noise levels from the transmission are as high as ever.

Mechanically, these Range Rovers are as easy to repair and maintain on a DIY basis as their forebears; but they are the last Range Rovers to be built before the introduction of sophisticated electrical systems put many repair and maintenance operations beyond the ability of the average DIY mechanic.

A loadspace cover was standard on 1985 Vogues and could be fitted optionally to other models.

These bodyside tapes were a new option for 1985, but did not prove popular.

THE 1986 RANGE ROVERS

The 1986 Range Rover model-year actually lasted from October 1985, when the new models were introduced, to December 1986, when the 1987 models arrived. It was the last year in which carburetted four-door models were built for the home market, and carburetted two-doors were built in only tiny numbers thereafter, mostly for overseas markets. Those who wanted two-door models generally opted for the new turbodiesel engine after its introduction in April 1986. Most of the 1986 Range Rovers attracted 'C'-suffix registrations in Great Britain; those registered after 1st August 1986 attracted 'D'-suffix registrations.

For the 1986 model-year, the best-selling Vogue models were equipped with the new fuel-injected 3.5-litre engine, and are thus outside the scope of this book. They were further distinguished by a front spoiler with twin driving lamps, plastic bumper end-caps and rubber bump-strips along the sides with a bright insert. These features were not found on other 1986 Range Rovers.

However, the few non-Vogue models which were sold during the 1986 season shared a number of revisions with the new fuel-injected Vogues. The engine itself was slightly more powerful than before, and there were substantial modifications to the transmissions. Five-speed models now had a new, short-stick, remote gearchange, while the old three-speed automatic had been replaced by a new four-speed type with a lock-up overdrive top gear, made by ZF in Germany. Dual-rate coil springs on the rear axle also reduced the Range Rover's characteristic body roll, and the rear dampers now both pointed in the same direction - forwards.

Land Rover had also introduced all-welded body frames for 1986. These eliminated the variations in size possible with the earlier bolted frames, and made for more consistent gaps between panels. Paint quality was also improved, and several new metallic finishes were introduced. The front doors on four-door models now had red door-open warning lamps in their edges, and puddle lamps in their lower faces. The whole of the lower dash area had been redesigned, and incorporated back-lit heater controls and an angled radio panel below them. This mated up to a redesigned console on the transmission tunnel, with a neater storage box between the seats. Interior trim, however, was still in Bronze Check, and both Silver Grey and the new Bracken velour were exclusive to Vogue models.

In December 1986, Land Rover announced a number of further revisions to the Range Rover, most of which had been designed to prepare it for its forthcoming launch in the USA. From this date, the fuel-injected engine was fitted to all four-door models for the UK market.

By the time of the 1986 models, the Vogue was taking such a high proportion of sales that both two-doors and ordinary four-doors like this were quite rare on the UK market. The headlamp guards seen here were not a standard fitment.

The Vogue model was taking such a high proportion of UK sales by the 1986 model-year that very few carburetted models were actually sold. Those which were are well worth having, as they incorporate a number of worthwhile improvements.

The revised rear suspension is a definite improvement, although body-roll on corners is still marked on 1986 Range Rovers. The slightly more powerful engine makes a minor contribution to driveability (though not noticeably to actual performance), but the real benefits lie in the revised transmissions. The remote gearshift on five-speed models gives the Range Rover an altogether car-like gearchange, and the four-speed automatic gearbox is altogether more responsive than the older three-speed type, as well as offering better fuel economy. However, probably not many carburetted 1986 Range Rovers had the ZF box.

This is the 1986 Vogue, now equipped with a fuel-injected engine and therefore outside the scope of this book. The rubber bump-strips on the bodysides and the front spoiler with its twin driving lamps are instant recognition features.

Five-speed models for 1986 had a new gearshift which improved the change quality considerably. The dashboard and console were also redesigned. This is in fact a Vogue model.

POLICE-SPECIFICATION RANGE ROVERS

Right from the beginning, Rover believed that the Range Rover would make a good Police vehicle, and a first demonstrator vehicle was prepared late in 1970. Police Review tested one and reported that it had "never come across such a universally-acceptable, or ready-made, Police vehicle as the Range Rover". Orders soon came in from several Forces in Britain, and the first Range Rovers entered Police service at the beginning of 1972. Thereafter, Police Range Rovers, finished in white with fluorescent red and yellow or red and blue side striping, became a familiar sight on motorway patrol duties. Several overseas Police Forces also took Range Rovers.

After September 1979, two-door Range Rovers used by the Police were mostly to the stripped-out Fleet Line specification, with Ambla leathercloth upholstery, PVC flooring, and no power steering. Some Police Forces in Britain had their vehicles fitted with Janspeed turbochargers to improve their ability as high-speed chase vehicles.

Four-door Range Rovers did not generally appear in Police livery until the mid-1980s, when production of the two-door models for the Home Market had effectively ceased. In general, these had the lowest specification available in order to minimise costs and thus, for example, had five-spoke steel wheels instead of the three-spoke alloy type.

No two Police Forces' requirements are identical, and the type and layout of extra equipment fitted to Police Range Rovers varied considerably. However, most had a split-charge electrical system with high-output alternator to power a radio receiver/transmitter, a calibrated speedometer in the middle of the dashboard, and various additional lights on the roof. Equipment was stowed on racks in the rear load area. Many ex-Police Range Rovers have found their way on to the second-hand market. Any white Range Rover in good mechanical condition in spite of an enormous mileage, with a basic specification and all sorts of unexplained holes in the dashboard, is likely to be an ex-Police model.

Two views of a typical Police-operated Range Rover. This example was put into service by London's Metropolitan Police in 1982. Note that the Fleet Line models, of which this is one, had the pre-1979 style of rear lights without the fog guard lamps (hence the extra units hung below the rear bumper) and had no head restraints. Nevertheless, the upholstery in this vehicle is cloth rather than Ambla.

Some export markets were provided with special versions of the Range Rover, mostly because of local motor vehicle legislation. A full list of specifications would be tedious; the following is intended to give a flavour of the differences in some export models.

CKD Assembly

In some markets, import regulations meant that motor vehicles had to have a certain percentage of locally-sourced components or that a certain percentage of local labour had to go into their assembly. For these markets, Solihull provided partially-built or kit-form Range Rovers, known as CKD (Completely Knocked Down) vehicles. By 1985, Range Rovers were being assembled from CKD kits in Kenya, Nigeria, Zaire and Zambia.

Engines

Different exhaust emissions standards in different markets meant that different versions of the 3.5-litre V8 engine had to be built. The most radically different versions were built for the Australian market, beginning in the late 1970s.

Germany

West German safety regulations had a marked effect on Range Rovers sold in that country. The vehicles had to have a driver's seat with an adjustable backrest, rubber bumper overriders with red reflectors at the rear (the reflector in the lamp unit was covered by a special V8 badge), and sleeves over the twin exhaust outlet pipes to remove their sharp edges.

Lighting

The peculiarities of vehicle lighting regulations in different export markets meant that several different headlamp types were fitted to Range Rovers. Some markets also required side repeater flashers, and these were eventually standardised on the 1980 models.

Range Rover Vans

Some European and Scandinavian markets took Range Rover Vans. These were based on two-door models and had either fixed rear side windows or plain metal panels in place of the sliding windows. No rear seats were fitted, and there was a half-height bulkhead behind the front seats. A few Range Rover Vans were also delivered to special order in the UK.

Range Rover Vans were made available for some overseas markets. This version had fixed side windows, but, of course, no rear seat. It was sold in Denmark during the 1970s. Note the silver bumpers and the side repeater flasher - a combination never found on production models for the home market.

MODIFICATIONS

The subject of Range Rover modifications is a huge one which is impossible to cover fully here. Generally speaking, it is possible to update the specification of an early Range Rover by fitting parts from a later vehicle, and this is often the simplest way of personalising a vehicle. There have also been many specialist aftermarket conversions, and probably many DIY conversions as well. Some of the more common modifications are discussed below. You might find some of them on a vehicle you intend to buy, or you might consider making them to your own vehicle. In either case, these notes are designed to help.

Bull bars. In the Australian outback, a strong 'roo bar across the front of a Range Rover is an essential accessory. Kangaroos have scant regard for motor vehicles and commonly jump out right in front of them; a 'roo bar is designed to ensure that minimum damage is done to the vehicle in the resulting impact. In Great Britain (where they are usually called bull bars), they are simply not necessary, and are best looked upon as a fashionable accessory. There is an argument which says that they make a vehicle look more aggressive. There is also one which says that, in a collision, a bull bar is likely to be bent against a Range Rover's bodywork

and cause more damage than the original impact would have caused by itself.

Diesel engines. Fuel economy has never been one of the Range Rover's strong points, and many owners have replaced a tired V8 petrol engine with a diesel unit in pursuit of cheaper motoring. The effectiveness of this depends partly on the engine used and partly on the competence with which the conversion has been carried out. There are several reputable conversion specialists who make a good job of such conversions. Home conversions, however, can be very much less satisfactory. Many conversions have used Perkins and Peugeot engines; more recently, high-speed diesels and turbodiesels from Mazda, Isuzu and Nissan have been favoured. Land Rover also introduced a VM turbocharged diesel as an option in the Range Rover during 1986, and in 1989 announced its own direct-injection turbodiesel for the related Discovery model; both of these engines can be persuaded to fit a Range Rover without much difficulty. Fuel economy with a diesel engine generally ranges between 25mpg and 35mpg - substantially better than with the original petrol engine. The drawbacks with the earlier types of engine are very much reduced performance (both in acceleration and top speed) and very much increased

Bull bars have proved a popular bolt-on accessory for Range Rovers, though their value in the UK is largely cosmetic.

A popular diesel conversion has used the British Perkins 4236 engine...

... but more recently, Japanese engines like this Mazda SL35TI have become popular.

noise levels. The drawback with the later types is the cost of the installation.

Gearbox conversions. The early four-speed manual gearbox has a number of disadvantages, and many owners have elected to replace it with the later five-speed type when renewal becomes necessary. The conversion is simple, straightforward and worthwhile. It is also possible to fit the much quieter Borg Warner chain-driven transfer box with viscous-coupled centre differential (introduced in 1988) in place of the LT230R or LT230T types. Schuler Presses carried out a number of transmission conversions, some adding automatic gearboxes and some adding a Voith chain-driven transfer box as part of an anti-lock braking system conversion.

Interior conversions. There is no reason why an early Range Rover should not be modified with seats and other interior parts from a later model, and many owners have done this. However, every conversion needs careful planning: for example, the "belt-less" front seats from 1985 and 1986 models cannot be used on earlier vehicles, because these have no provision for seat belt mountings in the body structure. Similarly, the transmission tunnel on five-speed models and automatics is narrower than on four-speed models, with the result that the later carpets and console panels need careful modification to fit an early vehicle. As the custom conversion specialists have demonstrated, there is no limit to what can be done with the interior of a Range Rover. However, cost can affect the issue and, when buying a Range Rover with a converted interior, it is always advisable to check how easily replacement items can be obtained if they are ever needed.

Performance conversions. The V8 engine used in the Range Rover has also been a favourite high-performance engine for road cars, and there is no shortage of tuning expertise or conversion parts to improve its performance. The main things to remember when examining a performance-tuned Range Rover are to assess how well the work has been carried out and to find out what the conversion was designed to achieve. Some high-performance conversions designed for road use can materially reduce the Range Rover's abilities off-road by adding top-end power at the expense of bottom-end torque. Many of them will also significantly increase fuel consumption, especially if you regularly make use of their higher performance.

Probably the simplest performance conversion of an early Range Rover is to replace its carburetted V8 with a fuel-injected 3.5-litre (165bhp) or 3.9-litre (185bhp) from a later model. But there is a lot more to these conversions than simply swopping engines, and relatively few such conversions have been carried out.

Range Rover engines have also been fitted with turbochargers (mainly by Janspeed), which give a performance boost at higher speeds without a fuel consumption penalty. However, some conversions also lack low-down torque, and there can be an irritating "kick in the back" as the turbocharger cuts in. Perhaps the most important thing with a turbocharged Range Rover is to ensure that the turbocharger has been properly maintained. Supercharger conversions also appeared in the late 1980s, but their cost has kept down the numbers of early Range Rovers fitted with them.

Schuler Presses (now Overfinch) have carried out many high-performance conversions using Chevrolet V8 engines in place of the Rover V8. These conversions are all excellently engineered; beware, however, of DIY imitations. In all high-performance Range Rover conversions, it is vital to ensure that suspension and braking modifications have been made where appropriate.

Suspension modifications. Some owners fit heavy-duty coil springs at the rear in order to prepare their vehicles for towing. Generally speaking, this is unnecessary, and simply results in a hard ride. Tougher springs all round have also been seen as a simple way of reducing body roll, but once again a hard ride is the penalty. Tougher springs can also raise the ride height, which in turn raises the Range Rover's centre of gravity and increases the chance that it will roll over in rough-terrain use or during over-enthusiastic cornering.

Range Rovers can be fitted with "handling kits", which reduce body-roll on the road and do not materially affect off-road ability. These kits depend mainly on anti-roll bars fitted to both axles. Early Range Rovers with such a kit will probably have the one developed by Harvey Bailey Engineering (also marketed, in further developed form, as the Warwick Banks handling kit). Land Rover introduced its own anti-roll bars on 1991 model-year Range Rovers and made a conversion kit available through Land Rover Parts. However, the kit is designed to fit 1986 model and later Range Rovers; earlier vehicles require chassis modifications before the kit can be fitted.

Wheel and tyre modifications. The standard tyres on Range Rovers throughout the period covered by this book were Michelin dual-purpose types,

Many owners have opted for aftermarket wheels.

Turbocharging has proved a popular way of extracting more performance from the existing 3.5 litre V8. This is a twin-turbo installation by Janspeed.

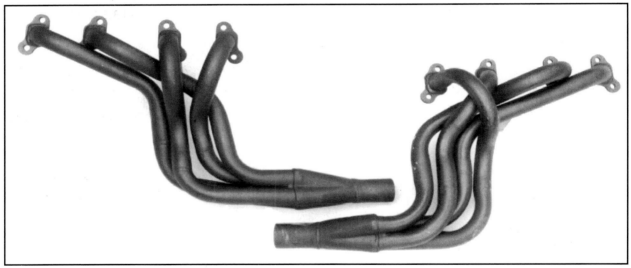

Also by Janspeed are these exhaust manifolds, which offer some performance gains for relatively little outlay.

which have good off-road characteristics. They are, however, a compromise tyre designed also to give a comfortable on-road ride. Tyres from Avon and Pirelli specified as original equipment on later Range Rovers are biased slightly more towards on-road use, but are generally adequate for most off-road use. Some owners who use their vehicles off-road a lot have fitted tyres which have excellent rough-terrain performance; however, all of them cause a deterioration of the on-road ride.

Cosmetic wheel modifications are a matter of taste: one popular type among Range Rover owners is a white-painted spoked wheel. However, there is no good reason to fit wide wheels and tyres, except for appearances' sake or for really heavy off-road work. Even then, you need to take care: the 1971 British Trans-Americas Expedition Range Rovers suffered repeated differential failures when using ultra-wide swamp tyres.

SPECIFICATIONS - HOME MARKET RANGE ROVERS

1971-1976 model years

Engine: 3,528cc (88.9mm bore x 71.1mm stroke) V8 petrol engine with 8.25:1 compression ratio; two Zenith-Stromberg CD2S carburettors; 130bhp at 5,000rpm and 185 lbs/ft of torque at 2,500rpm.

Transmission: Single-dry-plate clutch, 10.5in diameter. Four-speed and reverse LT95 gearbox; ratios 4.069:1, 2.448:1, 1.505:1, 1.00:1, reverse 3.664:1. Integral two-speed transfer box with 1.174:1 (high) and 3.32:1 (low) ratios. Lockable centre differential. Front and rear axle ratios 3.54:1.

Steering, suspension and brakes: Recirculating-ball, worm and nut steering with 18.2:1 ratio (20.55:1 ratio from autumn 1972). Live axles front and rear with coil springs and hydraulic telescopic dampers; front axle located by radius arms and Panhard rod; rear axle located by radius arms, support rods, and central wishbone assembly incorporating a Boge Hydromat self-energising ride-levelling strut. Hydraulic servo-assisted disc brakes, with dual line piping system; internal expanding drum-type parking brake operating on transfer box rear output shaft. 16-inch wheels with 205x16 tyres.

NOTES:

(1) The first 984 engines had an 8.5:1 compression ratio and gave 135bhp at 4,750rpm.

(2) The first 300 or so vehicles had a lockable limited-slip centre differential.

1977 model year

Transmission: High ratio in transfer box changed to 1.116:1.

1978-1979 model years

Engine: Compression ratio changed to 8.13:1; maximum power 132bhp at 5,000rpm; maximum torque 186 lbs/ft at 2,500rpm.

1980-1981 model years

Transmission: High ratio in transfer box changed to 1.113:1. Steering: Adwest Varamatic power-assisted steering with 17.5:1 ratio standardised (optional since January 1973).

NOTES:

(1) In Vogue limited-edition models only had the 9.35:1 compression engine and taller transfer box gearing standardised on 1982 models.

(2) The transfer box high ratio was changed to 1.222:1 late in 1980.

(3) Fleetline models were supplied without power-assisted steering.

1982 model year

Engine: Compression ratio changed to 9.35:1; two Zenith-Stromberg type 175 CD-SE carburettors; maximum power 125bhp at 4,000rpm; maximum torque 185 lbs/ft at 2,500rpm.

Transmission: High ratio in transfer box changed to 0.996:1.

1983 model year

Transmission: Optional torque converter automatic transmission with Chrysler Torqueflite A727 three-speed and reverse gearbox; ratios 2.45:1, 1.45:1, 1.00:1, reverse 2.20:1. Automatic models only had separate two-speed LT230R transfer gearbox with 1.003:1 (high) and 3.32:1 (low) ratios.

1984-1985 model years

Transmission: Five-speed and reverse LT77 gearbox replaced four-speed LT95 type; ratios 3.32:1, 2.13:1, 1.39:1, 1.00:1, 0.77:1, reverse 3.42:1. Five-speed models only had separate two-speed LT230R transfer gearbox with 1.19:1 (high) and 3.32:1 (low) ratios.

NOTE:

(1) All LT230R transfer boxes were superseded by LT230T types during the 1985 model-year. High ratio was 1.19:1 for both five-speed and automatic vehicles.

1986 model year

Engine: Maximum power 127bhp at 4,000rpm; maximum torque 194 lbs/ft at 2,500rpm. (Vogue models now fitted with fuel-injected engine).

Transmission: ZF type 4HP22 four-speed and reverse automatic gearbox replaced Chrysler three-speed type; ratios 2.47:1, 1.47:1, 1.00:1, 0.72:1, reverse 2.08:1.

V E H I C L E   I D E N T I F I C A T I O N

All Range Rovers have their chassis number stamped on a plate attached to the front body cross-member above the radiator grille. This plate is visible when the bonnet is opened.

On vehicles built before October 1979, the chassis number consists of nine digits. The first three are the type code; the next five are the serial number; and the final letter is a suffix which denotes design modifications which are of importance in servicing the vehicle. There is no method of telling from the chassis number when the vehicle was built, but the tables given below provide a guide.

Before February 1975 (approximately), each type code had its own serial number sequence, beginning with 00001; thereafter, a common sequence was used, but the distinctive individual type prefixes were retained.

Type codes were 355 (RHD, Home Market), 356 (RHD, Export), and 358 (LHD, Export). Small numbers of vehicles may also have been shipped CKD (Completely Knocked Down) in kit form for overseas assembly, but there are no records to confirm that this happened. In theory, the 357 sequence would have been allocated to RHD CKD vehicles, and the 359 sequence to LHD CKD vehicles. A typical chassis number from this era would be 35507301B.

Calendar year of manufacture	355 (RHD, Home)	356 (RHD, Export)	357 (LHD, Export)
1969	00001 to 00003	-	-
1970	00004 to 00312	00001 to 00005	00001 to 00006
1971	00313 to 03157	00006 to 00068	00007 to 00745
1972	03158 to 05718	00069 to 00820	00746 to 03227
1973	05719 to 08659	00821 to 01857	03228 to 05837
1974	08660 to 10572	01858 to 03156	05838 to 09850
1975	10573 to 11062	03157 to 03292	09851 to 10556

Calendar year of manufacture	All types
1975	12024 to 21662
1976	21663 to 31094
1977	31095 to 40479
1978	40480 to 55741
1979	55742 to 61821

On 1st November 1979 (October 1979 on the production lines), standardised 17-digit VIN (Vehicle Identification Number) codes were introduced. The serial numbers began again at 100001, and were preceded by a series of letters and numbers which contain the manufacturer's own code and details of the specification. These codes break down as follows:

SAL:	Land Rover Ltd (manufacturer's identity code)
LH:	Range Rover (model code)
A:	Additional model code letter to allow for variants (in practice, there are none)
B (etc):	Body type (A = Van, B = 2 -door, M = 4-door, R = Monteverdi)
V:	Engine type (V for low-compression carburetted V8, E for 9.35:1 high-compression carburetted V8)
2 (etc)	Steering and transmission (1 = RHD 4-speed manual, 2 = LHD 4-speed manual, 3 = RHD 3-speed automatic, 4 = LHD 3-speed automatic, 7 = RHD 5-speed manual, 8 = LHD 5-speed manual)
A (etc)	Major model change code (A until June 1984; B for 1985 models; C from October 1985)
A (etc)	Manufacturing plant (A = Solihull, F = CKD)

A typical VIN number from this period would be SALLHABV1AA101001.

Calendar year of manufacture	All types
1979	100001 to 102163
1980	102164 to 110584
1981	110585 to 119702
1982	119703 to 131429
1983	131430 to 143040
1984	143041 to 154589
1985	154590 to 167941
1986	167942 to 182600 (approx)

Engine numbers will be found on a ledge at the rear of the left-hand cylinder bank (very early models) or on a ledge beside the dipstick on the left-hand cylinder bank. Engine numbers consist of nine digits, made up of a three-digit type identifier, a five-digit serial number, and a suffix letter which identifies design modifications which affect service requirements. The type identifiers are as follows:

341	8.25:1 compression ratio, with Pulsair air injection system, for 4-speed manual gearbox; for German, Norwegian and Swedish markets
355	8.25:1 compression ratio, for 4-speed manual gearbox. (*Note:* all early Range Rover literature refers to the compression ratio as 8.5:1; but it fact only the first 984 A-suffix engines had 8.5:1 compression pistons). 8.13: 1

	compression ratio, with suffix F
359	8.25:1 compression ratio, CKD, for 4-speed manual gearbox
398	8.13:1 compression ratio, with Air Injection system for Australian market; for 4-speed manual gearbox
11D	9.35:1 compression ratio, with Pulsair air injection system, for 4-speed manual gearbox
13D	8.13:1 compression ratio, for 3-speed automatic gearbox
15D	9.35:1 compression ratio, with Pulsair air injection system, for 3-speed automatic gearbox
16D	9.35:1 compression ratio, with Pulsair air injection and Evaporation Loss Control; for Australian market
17D	9.35:1 compression ratio, with Pulsair air injection, for 5-speed manual gearbox
18D	8.13:1 compression ratio, for 5-speed manual gearbox
19D	9.35:1 compression ratio, with Pulsair air injection system for Australian market; for 5-speed manual gearbox
20D	8.13:1 compression ratio, with Pulsair air injection for Saudi Arabian market; for 5-speed manual gearbox
21D	8.13:1 compression ratio, with Pulsair air injection for Saudi Arabian market; for 3-speed automatic gearbox

Four-speed gearbox numbers will be found on the front face of the main gearbox (early examples) or on the rear face (late examples). On five-speed gearboxes, the number is stamped high up on the right-hand-side, near the front. Automatic gearboxes have their serial numbers on a plate attached to the outer casing. Identifying numbers are:

355	4-speed LT 95 with 1.174:1 high ratio (suffix A and B), 1.113:1 high ratio (suffix C), or 1.122:1 high ratio (suffix C from 35594060C)
12C	4-speed LT 95 with 0.996:1 high ratio (for use with 9.35:1 compression engine)
52A	5-speed LT 77
PK	3-speed Chrysler 727 automatic

Transfer boxes were integral with the main gearbox on 4-speed manual Range Rovers. On automatic and 5-speed models, however, the transfer box is a separate component. Identifying numbers are as follows:

14D	LT 230 R type, for use with 3-speed automatic
15D	LT 230 R type, for use with 5-speed manual
26D	LT 230 T type, for use with 3-speed automatic
27D	LT 230 T type, for use with 5-speed manual

Finally, axles also bear an identifying number, stamped on the casing to the left of the differential, looking forward with the axle on the vehicle. These numbers are:

355	Front axle, RHD
358	Front axle, LHD
355	Rear axle

Engine numbers are stamped on the pad next to the dipstick.

The chassis number of the Range Rover will be found on this plate which is attached to the front body cross-member.

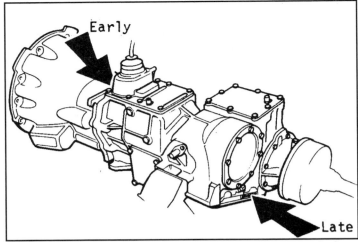

Gearbox numbers are on the front face of the box on early four-speeds, and on the rear face on later types.

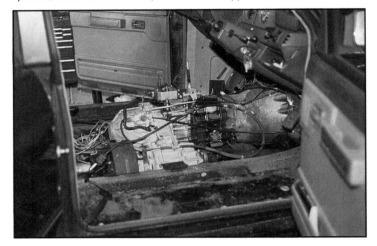

On five-speed gearboxes, the identifying numbers are on the right hand side, at the top.

Axles are also numbered, as arrowed.

SALES FIGURES

It is unfortunately not possible to quote accurate model-year production figures for Range Rovers at present. The figures which follow are therefore sales figures, which closely approximate to production figures but are not identical to them.

Until the end of 1974, the figures given represent sales between 1st September and 31st August the following year. The 1974-1975 figures are for the period between 1st September 1974 and 26th September 1975. The 1975-1976 figures cover sales between September 27th 1975 and December 31st 1976. All subsequent figures are for calendar-year sales.

Year	Annual total	Overall total
1969-1970	86	86
1970-1971	2,537	2,623
1971-1972	5,510	8,133
1972-1973	6,519	14,652
1973-1974	8,604	23,256
1974-1975	10,516	33,772
1975-1976	12,207	45,979
1977	9,667	55,646
1978	11,240	66,886
1979	11,373	78,529
1980	9,708	87,967
1981	10,441	98,408
1982	13,255	111,663
1983	12,182	123,845
1984	11,885	135,750
1985	13,458	149,188
1986	14,718	163,906

Standard paint colours for Range Rover models were available as shown below. Year figures refer to *model year,* which ran from autumn to autumn approximately: thus a 1971 model was one built between June 1970 and September 1971, a 1972 model was built between October 1971 and September 1972, and so on. An asterisk (*) denotes a metallic finish.

	71	72	73	74	75	76	77	78	79	80	81	82	83	84	85	86
(Blue colours)																
Caspian Blue*																86
Derwent Blue*														84	85	
Light Blue*										80	81					
Tasman Blue																86
Tuscan Blue	71	72	73	74	75	76	77	78	79	80	81	82				
Vogue Blue*											81	82	83			

Notes: Light Blue available on Monteverdi model only. Vogue Blue available only on In Vogue model in 1981, and only on four-door models thereafter.

	71	72	73	74	75	76	77	78	79	80	81	82	83	84	85	86
(Brown colours)																
Arizona Tan															85	86
Russet Brown										80	81	82	83	84	85	
Sahara Dust	71	72	73	74	75	76	77	78	79	80	81	82	83	84	85	
Savannah Beige*																86
Shetland Beige												82	83			
(Gold colours)																
Nevada Gold*													83	84	85	
(Green colours)																
Balmoral Green															85	86
Cypress Green*																86
Light Green*										80	81					
Lincoln Green	71	72	73	74	75	76	77	78	79	80	81	82	83	84		
Warwick Green										80	81					

Notes: Light Green available on Monteverdi models only. Lincoln Green available to special order only after 1981.

	71	72	73	74	75	76	77	78	79	80	81	82	83	84	85	86
(Grey colours)																
Anthracite*										80	81	82				
Cambrian Grey																86
Silver Grey*										80	81					

Note: Anthracite and Silver Grey available on Monteverdi models only.

	71	72	73	74	75	76	77	78	79	80	81	82	83	84	85	86
(Red colours)																
Masai Red	71	72	73	74	75	76	77	78	79	80	81	82				
Venetian Red												82	83	84	85	86
(Silver colours)																
Astral Silver*																86
Sierra Silver*													83	84	85	
Silver Birch*												82				
(Yellow colours)																
Bahama Gold	71	72	73	74	75	76	77	78	79							
Sandglow										80	81					
(White colours)																
Arctic White					75	76	77	78	79	80	81	82	83	84	85	
Chamonix White																86
Davos White	71	72	73	74												
White										80	81					

Note: White available on Monteverdi models only.

Interior trim

1970-1973 seasons:	Palomino PVC
1973-1975 seasons:	Palomino PVC; brushed nylon seat facings optional
1976-1979 seasons:	Palomino PVC; cloth seat facings optional; PVC front head restraints optional
1980 season:	Palomino cloth upholstery with PVC front head restraints standard
1980-1981 Monteverdi:	Black, Beige or Tan upholstery in cloth or pleated leather
1981-1984 seasons:	Bronze brushed velour upholstery standard; with matching headrests and detachable "velvet" cushions
1985 season:	Bronze Check cloth upholstery; Silver Grey velour on Vogue models only
1986 and later	Bronze Check cloth upholstery; Silver Grey or Bracken velour on Vogue(Efi) models only

MISCELLANEA

* After 1974, a number of specialist coachbuilding companies converted Range Rovers into luxury vehicles for the Midddle Eastern market. Almost anything that could be done to a Range Rover probably was done at some time; there were four-door bodies, convertibles, longer wheelbases, luxurious interiors, hydraulically-raised hunting seats, more powerful engines, automatic transmissions, wide wheels and anti-lock brakes, to name just a few. The main companies involved were Wood & Pickett, FLM Panelcraft, Glenfrome, Panther, Symbol, Rapport, Townley, Schuler Presses (neé Overfinch) and Vantagefield. Very few of these conversions remained in the UK.

* Range Rovers were also converted into six-wheel drive fire tenders by Carmichael. The third axle was not driven. Many such vehicles entered service with the RAF, bearing bodies and firefighting gear by Gloster Saro or HCB Angus. The Carmichael six-wheel chassis was also used as the basis of a luxury vehicle called the Clansman, aimed at the Middle East market.

* Scottorn produced a six-wheel Range Rover conversion with a driven third axle in the early 1980s.

* Carawagon produced a Range Rover caravan with an elevating roof in 1972, and also offered other caravan conversions. All remained rare.

* In March 1975, a specially converted Range Rover was put into service as a Royal Review vehicle for State occasions. This was joined in 1990 by a fuel injected Review vehicle.

* A 110-inch wheelbase chassis was developed in 1971 by Wadham Stringer in conjunction with the Rover Company. It was developed specifically to take an ambulance body, and both Wadham Stringer and Pilcher-Greene built such vehicles. Several have been converted privately into caravans after being withdrawn from ambulance duties.

* In 1971-1972, two left-hand-drive Range Rovers made the first ever land crossing of the Darien Gap (which divides North America from South America) as part of an 18,000-mile run from Alaska to Cape Horn. They were driven by British Army teams and both suffered repeated axle failures in the swamps of the Darien Gap as a result of being fitted with oversize tyres. Both vehicles still exist, in the BMIHT Collection.

The first State Review Range Rover entered service in 1975.

The first 6x4 fire tender was built by Carmichael in 1971, but the design remained almost unchanged by the time this example was built for the RAF in 1985. The scuttle side badging is not a throwback to the pre-1980 Range Rover, but actually bears the Carmichael name.

This ambulance on a 110-inch wheelbase was built for the Wiltshire Ambulance Service. The body was built by Wadham Stringer, who pioneered Range Rover ambulance conversions in the early 1970s.

The Middle Eastern taste for exotic vehicles led to innumerable conversions, such as this two-door convertible by Vantagefield of London.

Also aimed primarily at the Middle Eastern markets were these 6x6 conversions by Scottorn

One of the Range Rovers which made the first crossing of the Darien Gap, early in 1972.

The Rover Company and, later Land Rover Ltd, seem to have been reluctant to quote performance figures. Those quoted here have therefore been averaged out from the figures recorded by British motoring magazines during road tests, from owners' experiences and from the few "factory" figures available.

	Compression ratio	Max. speed	0-60 (secs)	30-50 in 4th gear	Average mpg
4-speed	9.25:1	96mph	14.2	10.0	15
4-speed and overdrive	8.13:1	96mph	14.3	12.2	17
4-speed	9.35:1	95mph	15.0	13.6	16
3-speed automatic	9.35:1	93.6mph	16.8	-	13
5-speed	9.35:1	96mph	14.4	15.2	17

Note: A collection of contemporary road test and other articles is published by Brooklands Books under the title *Range Rover Gold Portfolio 1970-1992*.

There are four basic types of car in the world.
And you can own all of them.

A luxury car.

An estate car.

A performance car.

A cross-country car.

Now you can drive four cars at once in the shape of our new Range Rover. You'll be the owner of a luxury car, a performance car, an estate car and a cross-country car.

First, a luxury car. We quote from our engineers' report: 'Driver and passenger comfort of a degree not previously obtained at anything like the price . . . superior suspension and internal appointments.'

Second, a performance car. The 3,528cc V8 engine gives a top speed of around 100 mph.

There's permanent four-wheel drive (usually only found on £7,000 cars) giving roadholding that out-classes most two-wheel drive cars.

Third, an estate car. With the back seat folded there's room for loads of up to 1,200 lbs. And the top half of the divided tail board is self-supporting, so you can safely leave it open when you're carrying extra long loads.

And fourth, a cross-country car. The chassis is as strong as a Land-Rover's. And like the Land-Rover the painted chassis and aluminium body panels resist rust and corrosion. The sturdy suspension, combined with an automatic ride-levelling device, gives an unbeatably smooth ride cross-country, laden or unladen. And a permanent four-wheel drive system makes it virtually impossible to get bogged down.

The Range Rover could be the answer if you're looking for one of the above four cars.

And if it so happens that you'd find all four quite useful, then the Range Rover is definitely the answer.

For the first time, you can have four cars under one roof.

RANGE ROVER

The Range Rover from Rover.
Recommended retail price £1,998 inc. P.T. (excluding delivery, number plates and seat belts)

The Rover Company Limited,
Solihull, Warwickshire

Technology made possible the car. Technology made possible the Range Rover.

A page for those interested in what happens under the bonnet.

3528 cc V8 engine The lightweight aluminium engine develops 156 bhp (gross) at 5000 rpm. And 8.5:1 compression ratio means 90 octane (2 star) petrol can be used. A four speed manual gearbox (fully synchromesh) with combined transfer gearbox gives eight forward and two reverse ratios. A gear for every situation.

Safety features There are disc brakes on all four wheels. The hand brake operates on the transmission – you can park safely on any normal 1 in 1 gradient. Other safety features include impact absorbing bodywork, dual braking system, collapsible steering column, radial tyres and a hazard flasher.

Chassis The box section chassis frame has the strength of a Land-Rover chassis (could anything be more tough or rugged?). The body panels are double skinned. The inner skin is steel-for safety. The outer is aluminium – to avoid rust problems.

Permanent four-wheel drive This has been achieved by incorporating a third differential between the two driving axles. This arrangement provides huge advantages under all road and most cross-country conditions. In exceptional off-road conditions the third differential can be locked (at the flick of a switch) to provide even better adhesion.

Ride-levelling device and suspension system A unique engineering development. The automatic ride-levelling device, and the sturdy beam axle and coil spring suspension combine to give you an unbeatably smooth ride. Not just on the road, but cross-country too. However heavy the load.

RANGE ROVER

The Range Rover from Rover.
Recommended retail price £1,998 inc. P.T.
(excluding delivery, number plates and seat belts)

The Rover Company Limited, Solihull, Warwickshire

Land Rover Owner — the only magazine for Land Rover & Range Rover enthusiasts.

Every month at newsagents, £2.10

or, available by subscription from
LRO PUBLICATIONS LTD.,
THE HOLLIES, BOTESDALE, DISS,
NORFOLK IP22 1BZ
at £25.00 for 12 Issues

Take an annual subscription and we will send you FREE either: an L.R.O. T-Shirt or a Magazine binder.

- Twelve Issues of Land Rover Owner for just £25.00 - post free and avoiding possible price increases.
- Free membership of LROC (Land Rover Owner Club) - personal membership card means many extra discounts.
- Send a cheque today and get the next 12 issues of your favourite magazine delivered to your door.
- Membership of the International Off-Road Club.

Please send me the next twelve issues of Land Rover Owner, starting with the........................ issue and enrol me as an LROC member.

I enclose cheque/PO for £25.00 (UK) ★

Charge my Visa/Access

a/c no. ....

Expiry Date ....

Send me a free ....
(enter choice of gift)

Post your complete form to:
LRO Publications Ltd.,
The Hollies, Botesdale,
Diss, Norfolk IP22 1BZ

Name ....

Address ....

....

....

Signed ....

Date ....

★ **Overseas rates available on request.**